THE INGREDIENTS OF AI

What Makes Intelligence Work

IntelliGloss AI Education Series

By

Susie Hala

IntelliGloss Press

Legal Disclaimer

Educational Purpose Disclaimer

"This publication is part of the IntelliGloss AI Education Series, a structured curriculum support system for AI literacy in grades 6–12."

The information presented in this publication is provided for educational and informational purposes only. This book is intended to support educators, administrators, parents, and learners in understanding the concepts, opportunities, and challenges associated with artificial intelligence in education. It is not intended to serve as legal, technical, policy, cybersecurity, or professional advice.

Readers should consult qualified professionals, institutional guidelines, and local regulations before implementing any educational programs, technologies, or policies described in this book.

Technology and Accuracy Disclaimer

Artificial intelligence is a rapidly evolving field. While every effort has been made to ensure the accuracy and reliability of the information presented at the time of publication, technologies, policies, research findings, and best practices may change over time. The author and publisher make no guarantees that all information will remain current or applicable in future technological environments.

Readers are encouraged to verify tools, platforms, and recommendations independently before using them in educational settings.

Implementation Responsibility

Schools, educators, and institutions are solely responsible for determining how and whether to implement artificial intelligence tools, strategies, or classroom activities discussed in this book. Educational environments vary widely, and policies regarding technology use, student privacy, and curriculum development differ by district, state, and country.

The author and publisher assume no responsibility for outcomes resulting from the implementation of ideas, examples, or frameworks described in this book.

Student Safety and Data Privacy

Artificial intelligence tools may involve the collection or processing of data. Educators and institutions are responsible for ensuring that any technology used complies with applicable student privacy laws, data protection regulations, and school policies, including but not limited to FERPA, COPPA, GDPR, or other relevant regulations depending on jurisdiction.

The author and publisher are not responsible for the privacy practices, security policies, or data handling procedures of third-party platforms or software mentioned in this book.

Third-Party Tools and References
This book may reference third-party technologies, organizations, research studies, or platforms for illustrative and educational purposes. Such references do not constitute endorsements or guarantees regarding the performance, reliability, safety, or suitability of those tools for educational use.

Educators and institutions should conduct their own evaluations and risk assessments before adopting any technology.

No Professional Liability
The author and publisher shall not be held liable for any direct, indirect, incidental, or consequential damages resulting from the use or misuse of the information contained in this book. This includes but is not limited to decisions related to curriculum design, technology adoption, classroom instruction, institutional policies, or educational outcomes.

Educational Interpretation
The concepts and examples provided in this book are intended to support discussion and learning. They should not be interpreted as official standards, mandatory guidelines, or universally applicable policies for artificial intelligence education.

Schools and educators are encouraged to adapt the ideas presented here according to their local policies, cultural context, educational standards, and student needs.

Author's Intent
The goal of this book is to promote responsible AI literacy, thoughtful discussion, and ethical awareness as schools prepare students for a world increasingly shaped by intelligent technologies.

The author encourages readers to approach artificial intelligence education with curiosity, caution, and a commitment to responsible learning.

Title: THE INGREDIENTS OF AI What Makes Intelligence Work

ISBN: 978-1-972925-09-6

Published by
IntelliGloss Press
United States of America

Dedication

This book is dedicated to the next generation of learners—
the students who will grow up in a world shaped by intelligent technology,
and who deserve to understand it with clarity, confidence, and purpose.

To the educators who show up every day with dedication and heart,
guiding students through a rapidly changing world—
your role has never been more important.

To the parents and families who support learning at home,
encouraging curiosity, responsibility, and growth—
you are the foundation of every child's success.

And to my granddaughters,
whose curiosity, imagination, and future inspire me to do this work—
this book is for you.

May you not only learn how to use technology,
but understand it, question it, and shape it for the good of others.

About the Author

Susie Hala
Founder of the IntelliGloss AI Education Series

Susie Hala is an author, educator, and curriculum developer dedicated to advancing artificial intelligence literacy in education. Her work focuses on helping schools, educators, and students understand how intelligent technologies are shaping modern society—and why that understanding is essential for the next generation.

Hala is the creator of the IntelliGloss AI Education Series, a comprehensive and growing collection of educational books designed to make complex artificial intelligence concepts accessible, structured, and practical for classroom use. Her work emphasizes clarity, organization, and responsible implementation, enabling schools to introduce AI literacy without requiring advanced technical backgrounds.

In addition to her work in education, Hala brings hands-on experience working with artificial intelligence systems, including early exposure to rule-based AI technologies during her time working with AT&T. She has also developed modern digital platforms that integrate artificial intelligence, automation, and online systems, building e-commerce solutions and AI-driven applications that connect payment platforms, hosting environments, and conversational AI tools into real-world, functional systems.

This combination of foundational understanding and practical experience allows her to translate complex AI concepts into clear, accessible language for both educators and students.

Recognizing that artificial intelligence is rapidly transforming how information is created, interpreted, and used, Hala advocates for equipping students with the ability not only to use AI tools, but to understand, question, and evaluate them. Her work emphasizes critical thinking, ethical awareness, and responsible digital citizenship.

The IntelliGloss AI Education Series supports schools in teaching key areas such as artificial intelligence foundations, algorithms, machine learning concepts, and AI ethics, as well as the broader evolution of intelligent systems—from Artificial Narrow Intelligence (ANI) to Artificial General Intelligence (AGI) and Artificial Superintelligence (ASI). These resources are designed for students in grades 6–12 and for educators seeking structured, classroom-ready approaches to AI literacy.

In addition to her work in education publishing, Hala has a strong background in entrepreneurship, having built and managed multiple businesses and educational initiatives. Her experience across industries reinforces her belief that technology education must remain grounded in human values, critical thinking, and ethical responsibility.

Her mission is clear: to ensure that the next generation understands intelligent technology—not just how to use it, but how it truly works.

Preface

Two Students. Two Paths. One Future.

Before we begin, it is important to understand why learning how artificial intelligence works—not just how to use it—matters for every student.

Imagine two students who have just graduated from high school and are preparing for a job interview. The first student knows how to use artificial intelligence tools. This student can generate answers, complete assignments quickly, and rely on AI to assist with tasks. However, this student does not understand how artificial intelligence works behind the scenes.

The second student also knows how to use AI tools, but in addition, understands the foundational concepts behind them. This student has learned about data, algorithms, tokens, models, and how intelligent systems are trained and operate. This student can think critically about AI, recognize its limitations, and adapt when needed.

At first, the first student may appear faster and more efficient. However, over time, the second student demonstrates a deeper level of understanding, independence, and problem-solving ability. The second student is not only able to use artificial intelligence but also to question it, improve it, and grow with it.

This book is written for the second student.

In a world where artificial intelligence is becoming part of everyday life, students must not only learn how to use intelligent systems—they must learn how they work. True understanding leads to confidence, responsibility, and the ability to lead in an AI-driven future.

This perspective is not just theoretical—it is personal.

There was a time when I was the first student.

I knew how to use systems. I followed processes, completed tasks, and worked within structured environments that required accuracy and consistency. At the time, I did not think of these systems as artificial intelligence. They were simply part of the job—tools that had to be learned, followed, and mastered.

But looking back, I now understand something much deeper. I was working within rule-based systems—the earliest foundation of what we now recognize as artificial intelligence.

That realization changed everything.

As I began studying modern AI, including machine learning, deep learning, and intelligent systems, I started to see a clear connection between the past and the present. The structured systems I once worked in, the logic behind decision-making, and the step-by-step processes all still exist today. They have simply evolved.

Artificial intelligence did not appear overnight. It grew from rule-based systems into systems that can now learn, adapt, and assist in ways we never imagined.

I made a decision to move from simply using systems to understanding them.

That journey—from student one to student two—is the reason these books exist.

My mission is to help others bridge that same gap.

I believe that artificial intelligence should be understandable for everyone. It should not feel intimidating or out of reach. Students should feel confident exploring it. Teachers should feel prepared to introduce it. Everyday learners should have access to clear, structured explanations that make sense.

You do not need a background in technology. You do not need to know how to code. You only need the right explanation.

A Note from the Author

AI Is a Tool — Not a Decision Maker

Artificial Intelligence is becoming part of everyday life. Students use it to complete assignments, teachers use it to support instruction, and businesses use it to improve efficiency. While these tools are powerful and useful, there is an important truth that must remain clear from the very beginning:

Artificial Intelligence does not make decisions—people do.

One of the main purposes of this book is to help readers understand how AI works, what it can do, and—just as importantly—what it cannot do. AI systems are designed to process information, identify patterns, and generate responses based on data. They can assist with thinking, but they do not think independently. They can provide answers, but they do not understand consequences. They can suggest ideas, but they do not choose actions.

Every outcome that involves AI begins and ends with human involvement. A person asks the question. A person reviews the response. A person decides what to do next. Responsibility does not transfer to the machine.

In today's world, it is easy to confuse speed with intelligence and automation with authority. Because AI can respond quickly and confidently, it may appear as though it is making decisions. In reality, it is performing a task based on patterns it has learned—not exercising judgment.

This distinction matters. When people begin to rely on AI without understanding its role, they risk misunderstanding information, misusing technology, or placing trust in a system that is not capable of accountability. Clear understanding leads to responsible use.

This book was written to remove confusion and provide clarity. It is designed to help students and educators move beyond simply using AI tools and begin understanding the structure behind them. By learning how AI supports human thinking—rather than replacing it—readers can approach technology with confidence, awareness, and responsibility.

Artificial Intelligence is a powerful assistant. It can enhance learning, support creativity, and improve productivity. But it remains a tool.

The decisions, the actions, and the responsibility will always belong to the human.

— Susie Hala

Bringing Clarity to Artificial Intelligence

During a recent meeting with a school district, it became clear that one of the biggest challenges in artificial intelligence education is not the technology itself—but the way it is explained.

In that discussion, terms such as **chatbots, generative AI, agentic AI, autonomy, tools, hallucinations, and AI usage levels** were all mentioned together. While each term represents a distinct concept, they were often blended into one conversation without clear distinctions. The result was confusion, even among those who were actively trying to understand and make informed decisions.

This experience revealed an important truth:
Without clear definitions and structure, artificial intelligence becomes difficult to teach, difficult to learn, and difficult to use responsibly.

This book is designed to provide that structure.

Understanding the Core Concepts

To build a strong foundation, it is essential to separate and define the key ideas that are often confused.

Chatbot
A chatbot is a conversational interface that allows users to interact with an AI system through questions and prompts. It responds to input but does not act beyond what is directly requested.

Generative AI (Gen AI)
Generative AI refers to systems that create new content, including text, images, audio, and code. These systems generate outputs based on patterns learned from large datasets. While powerful, generative AI does not truly understand information and may occasionally produce inaccurate results.

Agentic AI
Agentic AI describes systems that can take action toward a goal. Rather than responding to a single prompt, these systems can plan, make decisions within defined limits, and carry out multi-step tasks. This introduces a higher level of functional independence.

Autonomy
Autonomy refers to how independently an AI system operates. Some systems require constant human guidance, while others can perform multiple steps with minimal input. Autonomy is not a separate type of AI, but a measure of how much control the system has in completing tasks.

Additional Terms That Shape Understanding

AI Tools
AI tools are the applications people use to interact with artificial intelligence, such as writing assistants, design platforms, and data analysis systems. These tools make AI accessible in everyday tasks.

Hallucination
A hallucination occurs when an AI system generates information that appears correct but is inaccurate or unsupported. This is a known limitation of generative systems and highlights the need for human verification.

The AI Use Continuum

Another important concept is how AI is used at different levels. Rather than viewing AI as a single capability, it is more accurate to understand it as a continuum of use:

Assistive Use
AI supports simple tasks such as answering questions, correcting grammar, or providing suggestions.

Augmented Use
AI helps expand human capability by generating ideas, organizing content, and assisting in problem-solving.

Agentic Use
AI begins to take on multi-step responsibilities, planning and completing tasks with reduced human input.

This continuum shows that AI can range from a helpful assistant to a more independent system, depending on how it is applied.

The Moment Everything Sounded Like One Conversation

During a recent discussion on artificial intelligence, I listened closely as different experts spoke about the future of AI. One referenced advanced systems beyond human intelligence, another discussed goal-driven AI systems, and the conversation shifted quickly between topics like autonomy, tools, and system behavior. At first, it sounded like a single, unified discussion. But the more I listened, the more I realized something important.

They were not all talking about the same thing.

One part of the conversation focused on future possibilities—high-level systems that do not yet exist. Another part focused on current technologies that are already being used today. At the same time, different terms were being used to describe how AI behaves, how it makes decisions, and how much independence it may have. These ideas were layered together in a way that made them sound connected, even when they were not.

This experience revealed a major challenge in understanding artificial intelligence today. Many discussions combine different types of AI, different levels of intelligence, and different behaviors into one conversation. Without clear structure, these ideas begin to blur together. For someone trying to learn, this can feel overwhelming and confusing.

This book is built to solve that problem.

Artificial intelligence is not one single concept. It is a system made up of multiple layers. Some layers describe how intelligent a system is. Other layers describe how the system behaves. Still others describe how much control or independence the system has. When these layers are separated and explained clearly, AI becomes much easier to understand.

The goal of this book is to bring clarity where confusion often exists. Instead of mixing everything into one explanation, each concept is presented in a structured and organized way. This allows students, educators, and readers to see how the pieces fit together without losing sight of what each part actually means.

Understanding artificial intelligence begins with understanding its structure.

Once that structure is clear, the conversation becomes clearer as well.

Why Clarity Matters

When these concepts are not clearly defined, they merge into what can be described as a "conceptual blur." This can lead to misunderstandings about what AI can and cannot do, as well as unrealistic expectations or misuse in educational settings.

Clear understanding helps ensure that:

Students remain active learners, not passive users

Educators maintain control over instructional outcomes

AI is used as a support tool rather than a replacement for thinking

The Purpose of This Book

This book is built on a simple but essential principle:

Students should not only use artificial intelligence—they should understand it.

By clearly defining core concepts such as chatbots, generative AI, agentic AI, autonomy, and the continuum of AI use, this curriculum provides a structured pathway for developing both technical understanding and critical thinking.

Artificial intelligence is not a single tool or system. It is a collection of capabilities that must be understood in context.

Clarity is the foundation of responsible innovation.

The IntelliGloss Instructional Approach

The IntelliGloss AI Education Series is designed to help students move beyond simply using AI tools and begin understanding artificial intelligence as a complete system.

Students learn how AI is built, how it operates, and how it connects to the real world.

A Message to Students and Readers

If you have ever felt that technology was too complicated…
If you have ever been confused by systems that were never clearly explained…

I want you to know:

You are capable of understanding artificial intelligence.

Sometimes, the challenge is not the concept itself—it is how it has been presented.

This series was created to change that.

A Message to Educators

To the educators using this material:

These books are designed to support you in introducing artificial intelligence in a way that is clear, structured, and meaningful for students.

AI is becoming part of every industry, and students deserve more than just exposure to tools—they deserve understanding.

This series aims to provide that foundation.

Final Reflection

Every experience we have—especially the challenging ones—prepares us for something greater.

The systems I once worked in taught me discipline, structure, and attention to detail. Today, those same lessons allow me to break down complex ideas and make them understandable for others.

That is what this series represents:

Turning complexity into clarity.

Why Artificial Intelligence Education Matters for Every Student

Why AI Literacy Is Essential for Every Student

Artificial intelligence is no longer a future concept or a specialized technology used only by experts. It is already part of everyday life for students of all ages. From smartphones and search engines to navigation apps, social media, streaming platforms, and educational tools, AI systems influence how information is accessed, decisions are made, and learning takes place.

Because AI is embedded in daily life, understanding it is no longer optional. It is a foundational skill, similar to digital literacy and critical thinking. Students do not need to become programmers or engineers, but they do need to understand what AI is, how it works at a basic level, and how it affects their lives.

AI education should not be limited to computer science classrooms. Every student interacts with AI systems daily. Teaching students how these systems function empowers them to become informed users rather than passive consumers of technology.

This book is designed to make artificial intelligence understandable, approachable, and relevant. It focuses on clarity, responsibility, and real-world understanding to help students prepare for a future where humans and intelligent systems work side by side.

IntelliGloss AI Education Series

Teaching how AI actually works—from hardware to power to global systems.

Why AI Education Matters

Artificial intelligence is already shaping how students learn, write, research, and solve problems.

Yet many students—and educators—are using AI tools without understanding how these systems actually work.

Schools need more than access to technology.
They need structured, responsible AI education.

Our Approach

The IntelliGloss AI Education Series is designed to help students move beyond simply using AI tools and begin understanding artificial intelligence as a complete system.

Students learn how AI is built, how it operates, and how it connects to the real world.

The IntelliGloss Framework

Our books introduce AI through a clear and connected system:

Chip Family — the hardware that powers AI

Watts Family — the rate at which AI uses power

Energy Family — the total power AI consumes over time

Infrastructure Family — the global systems that support AI

This framework helps students understand AI from the inside out.

Built for the Classroom

Each book includes:

Structured chapters aligned with semester learning

Clear explanations designed for student understanding

Reflection sections with learning objectives

Worksheets, quizzes, and answer keys

Teacher Implementation Guides

Supporting Schools and Educators

The IntelliGloss series supports:

Responsible and ethical AI use

Student data awareness and safety

Critical thinking and digital literacy

Classroom-ready instruction for grades 6–12 and beyond

What This Book Is—and What It Is Not

Many people today are becoming familiar with artificial intelligence through tools like ChatGPT, Microsoft Copilot, Canva, and other AI-powered applications. These tools can help with writing, answering questions, creating images, and completing everyday tasks.

In addition to these tools, you may also hear terms such as **AI agents, agentic AI, autonomous systems, and generative AI**. While these may sound complex, they are all part of the same evolving landscape of artificial intelligence technologies.

This book is not a guide on how to use those tools.

Instead, it explains what makes those tools possible.

Behind every AI tool is a system made up of multiple layers working together. At the most basic level, information is represented as bits and processed through powerful computer chips. That information is organized into data, broken into tokens, and then processed by algorithms and models that allow the system to recognize patterns, generate responses, and perform tasks.

These components—chips, bits, tokens, data, algorithms, and models—work together as a complete system. While users may only see the tool, the real intelligence comes from how these underlying parts interact behind the scenes.

Artificial intelligence can also be understood in terms of different levels of capability. Most of the AI systems used today fall under **Artificial Narrow Intelligence (ANI)**, which is designed to perform specific tasks, such as answering questions or generating content. More advanced forms, such as **Artificial General Intelligence (AGI)** and **Artificial Superintelligence (ASI)** represent future possibilities where AI could match or exceed human-level thinking. While these advanced levels are still theoretical, understanding the differences helps provide a broader view of where AI is today and where it may be heading.

For students, parents, and educators, this distinction is important. Learning how to use AI tools is helpful, but understanding how they work—and where they fit within the larger AI landscape—builds stronger thinking, better decision-making, and more responsible use.

Most importantly, artificial intelligence does not make decisions on its own. It does not take responsibility for actions or outcomes. AI systems generate responses based on data and patterns, but it is always the human who decides what to do with that information.

This book is designed to make these underlying systems clear and accessible, even for readers who are new to artificial intelligence.

Artificial intelligence is still in its early stages of development. As these technologies continue to grow, those who understand the foundation behind them will be better prepared to adapt, question, and use them wisely.

Who This Book Is For

This book is designed for educators, school leaders, and curriculum developers guiding students in an age of rapidly advancing technology.

Artificial intelligence is already influencing how students learn, research, and communicate. Yet many educators have not received formal training in how these systems work or how they should be addressed in the classroom.

This book helps bridge that gap by providing clear explanations and practical frameworks for understanding artificial intelligence in an educational setting.

How Schools Can Use This Book

This book supports schools in developing a structured approach to artificial intelligence literacy.

It can be used for:

- Professional development for educators
- Classroom discussions and activities
- Curriculum support across subject areas
- Policy and academic integrity conversations

Rather than focusing on specific tools, this book emphasizes lasting principles that help students understand, evaluate, and use AI responsibly.

Closing Perspective

Artificial intelligence will continue to evolve. With the right knowledge and leadership, schools can ensure that students not only use these technologies, but understand them, question them, and apply them responsibly.

IntelliGloss is more than a book series. It is a structured approach to preparing students for a future shaped by artificial intelligence.

Rather than focusing only on how to use AI tools, this series helps students understand how AI actually works—from its foundational building blocks to real-world applications.

"Before exploring the technical structure of artificial intelligence, it is equally important to understand the human principles that guide its use."

Human Values Family

Definition

The Human Values Family in artificial intelligence represents the guiding principles that shape how AI systems are created, used, and integrated into society. These values include ethics, responsibility, trust, and human well-being.

Artificial intelligence may be built on data, algorithms, and computational systems, but its true impact is measured by how it affects people. For this reason, AI is not only a technical system—it is a human-centered system.

Key Concepts

The Human Values Family exists to ensure that artificial intelligence serves humanity in a positive and responsible way. While AI systems can process information and generate outcomes, they do not possess judgment, empathy, or moral understanding.

This means that human values must guide every stage of AI development—from design to deployment.

AI reflects the intentions, decisions, and assumptions of the people who build and use it. If those values are not carefully considered, AI systems can unintentionally produce biased, harmful, or misleading results.

Understanding human values in AI is not optional—it is essential.

Core Elements of the Human Values Family

Ethics
Ethics in AI refers to making decisions that are fair, just, and respectful of human rights. This includes minimizing bias, protecting privacy, and ensuring transparency in how systems operate.

Responsibility
Responsibility means that humans remain accountable for AI systems. Developers, educators, organizations, and users must take ownership of how AI is used and the outcomes it produces.

Trust
Trust is critical for the successful adoption of AI. People must feel confident that AI systems are reliable, safe, and aligned with their best interests.

Human Well-Being
AI should enhance human life—not replace, harm, or diminish it. This includes supporting learning, improving access to information, and creating opportunities while maintaining human dignity.

Real-World Connection

Artificial intelligence is already influencing how people learn, communicate, and make decisions. From search engines to classroom tools, AI is shaping daily experiences.

Without clear human values guiding these systems, there is a risk of reinforcing misinformation, bias, or unrealistic expectations.

For students, this means learning not only how to use AI tools, but how to question them, evaluate their outputs, and understand their limitations.

Applications in Education

In the classroom, the Human Values Family helps students develop critical thinking and ethical awareness. Teachers can use this framework to guide discussions about fairness, responsibility, and the impact of technology on society.

Students can explore questions such as:

How should AI be used responsibly?

What makes an AI system fair?

How does technology influence human behavior?

This approach supports both technical understanding and responsible decision-making.

Benefits

Teaching human values in AI helps students:

Develop ethical awareness

Strengthen critical thinking

Understand the societal impact of technology

Become responsible users and future creators of AI

It ensures that learning about AI goes beyond functionality and includes responsibility.

Challenges

Human values are not always universal. Different cultures, communities, and individuals may have different perspectives on what is considered fair or ethical.

Additionally, AI technology is evolving rapidly, often faster than policies and guidelines can keep up. This makes it essential for educators and students to stay informed and adaptable.

Summary

The Human Values Family reminds us that artificial intelligence is not just about machines—it is about people.

By focusing on ethics, responsibility, trust, and human well-being, students can learn to use AI thoughtfully and responsibly.

Understanding these principles helps prepare learners to navigate a world where artificial intelligence plays an increasingly important role in everyday life.

Executive Summary

IntelliGloss AI Education Series

Teaching How Artificial Intelligence Actually Works

Artificial intelligence is already shaping how students learn, write, research, and make decisions. Yet in many classrooms, students are being introduced to AI tools without understanding how these systems actually function.

This creates a critical gap.

Students may become efficient users of technology, but without foundational knowledge, they are not equipped to think critically, evaluate outputs, or use AI responsibly. As AI continues to expand across every industry, this gap will only grow more significant.

The **IntelliGloss AI Education Series** was created to address this challenge.

The Problem

Most current approaches to AI in education focus on tool usage rather than system understanding. As a result:

- Students rely on AI without understanding its limitations
- Educators lack structured frameworks for teaching AI concepts
- Key terms such as generative AI, agentic AI, and autonomy are often introduced without clear definitions

Responsibility and ethical use are not consistently emphasized

Without clarity, artificial intelligence becomes difficult to teach, difficult to learn, and difficult to manage in a school environment.

The Solution

The IntelliGloss AI Education Series provides a structured, classroom-ready approach to artificial intelligence literacy for grades 6–12.

Rather than focusing on individual tools, this series teaches students how AI works as a complete system—from foundational components to real-world applications.

Students learn to move beyond surface-level interaction and develop true understanding.

The IntelliGloss Framework

The series introduces AI through a clear and connected structure, including:

Foundational building blocks such as data, algorithms, tokens, and models

System-level understanding through categories such as intelligence level, behavior, and control

Real-world context through applications, limitations, and responsible use

Human-centered learning through ethics, responsibility, trust, and student safety

This structured approach transforms artificial intelligence from a confusing concept into an understandable system.

Instructional Design

Each book in the series is designed for practical classroom use and includes:

Structured chapters aligned with instructional pacing

Clear, student-friendly explanations

Reflection sections to reinforce understanding

Worksheets, quizzes, and answer keys

Teacher implementation support

No prior technical background is required for educators or students.

Guiding Principle

A central message of the IntelliGloss series is:

Artificial Intelligence is a tool—not a decision maker.

Students learn that while AI can support thinking and provide information, all decisions, actions, and responsibilities remain with humans. This principle reinforces critical thinking, accountability, and responsible technology use.

Why It Matters

AI literacy is no longer optional. It is a foundational skill.

Students who understand how AI works will be better prepared to:

Think critically about information

Adapt to emerging technologies

Use AI responsibly and ethically

Succeed in an increasingly AI-driven world

Our Goal

The IntelliGloss AI Education Series is designed to help schools move beyond simply using artificial intelligence tools and toward a deeper understanding of how these systems actually work.

By providing clear structure, defined concepts, and real-world context, this series equips students and educators with the knowledge needed to think critically, evaluate information, and use AI responsibly.

The goal is not just to introduce technology—but to build understanding, confidence, and accountability in an AI-driven world.

This is not just about learning to use AI—it is about preparing students to understand it, question it, and lead with it.

Clarity leads to confidence.
Understanding leads to responsible use.

Mission Statement

The mission of the IntelliGloss AI Education Series is to make artificial intelligence clear, structured, and accessible for every student and educator.

In a world where AI is rapidly transforming how information is created, used, and understood, this series is designed to move beyond surface-level interaction and provide a deeper understanding of how intelligent systems actually work.

Through clear explanations, organized frameworks, and real-world context, IntelliGloss equips learners with the ability to think critically, evaluate information, and engage with technology responsibly.

This mission is grounded in a simple belief:
students should not only learn how to use artificial intelligence—they should understand it.

By building both technical awareness and human-centered understanding, the IntelliGloss AI Education Series prepares students to navigate, question, and shape a future increasingly influenced by intelligent technologies.

The goal is not just to keep up with artificial intelligence—but to understand it, guide it, and use it responsibly.

Vision Statement

The vision of the IntelliGloss AI Education Series is to create a future where artificial intelligence is clearly understood, responsibly used, and thoughtfully integrated into education and everyday life.

In this future, students are not passive users of technology, but informed thinkers who understand how intelligent systems work, recognize their limitations, and apply them with purpose and responsibility.

Educators are equipped with clear frameworks and structured resources that make artificial intelligence accessible, teachable, and meaningful across all subjects—not just in technical fields.

Schools become environments where technology is not simply adopted, but understood—where students are encouraged to question, evaluate, and engage with AI in ways that support learning, creativity, and ethical awareness.

As artificial intelligence continues to evolve, this vision supports a generation that is prepared not only to adapt to change, but to lead it with knowledge, confidence, and integrity.

The future of artificial intelligence will not be defined by technology alone—but by the understanding and responsibility of those who use it.

Connecting AI Understanding to Cybersecurity Awareness

Definition

Understanding artificial intelligence is the first step toward understanding cybersecurity. While cybersecurity focuses on protecting systems, data, and users, artificial intelligence explains how those systems are built, how they function, and where they may be vulnerable.

The Connection

Every AI system is made up of components such as data, algorithms, models, and infrastructure. These same components are also the targets of cybersecurity threats.

When students understand:

How data is collected and stored

How algorithms make decisions

How AI models process information

How systems operate across frontend and backend layers

They begin to recognize where risks can exist and how systems can be misused.

Why This Matters

In today's digital world, students are not just users of technology—they are participants in complex systems powered by artificial intelligence.

Without understanding how these systems work:

Technology becomes something they trust without question

Risks become harder to recognize

Decisions are made without awareness of consequences

With understanding:

Students become more aware of how their data is used

They recognize how systems can be manipulated

They make more informed and responsible choices

Building Digital Readiness

Digital readiness is not only about using tools. It is about understanding the systems behind those tools.

By learning how AI works, students develop:

Awareness of digital environments

Confidence in navigating technology

A foundation for future learning, including cybersecurity

Conclusion

Cybersecurity begins with understanding.

Before students can protect systems, they must first understand how those systems are built and how they operate. This is why learning artificial intelligence is not only about innovation—it is also about responsibility.

The Foundation of Artificial Intelligence

Definition

The foundation of Artificial Intelligence (AI) refers to the core building blocks that allow AI systems to function. These building blocks work together to help machines learn from information, recognize patterns, and make decisions. AI is not magic—it is a system built on structured components that operate behind the scenes.

Understanding the Foundation in Simple Terms

Artificial Intelligence can be compared to a house. Before a house is complete, it must be built on a strong foundation. This foundation includes concrete, wiring, plumbing, and support structures that are not always visible but are essential for the house to function properly.

In the same way, AI systems rely on foundational components that are not visible to users but are necessary for AI tools to work. When people use AI applications such as chatbots or design tools, they are interacting with the surface. The true power of AI comes from what is underneath.

Key Components of the AI Foundation

1. Data (The Information)

Data is the starting point of all AI systems. It includes text, images, numbers, audio, and other forms of information. AI systems learn by analyzing patterns within this data.

2. Algorithms (The Instructions)

Algorithms are step-by-step instructions that tell the AI system how to process data. They guide how the system learns, identifies patterns, and produces results.

3. Models (The Trained System)

A model is created when data and algorithms are combined through a training process. The model acts as the "brain" of the AI system, allowing it to make predictions and generate responses.

4. Computing Power (The Engine)

AI systems require powerful computers to process large amounts of data. This includes specialized hardware such as processors and graphics processing units (GPUs) that allow AI to function efficiently.

5. Infrastructure (The Environment)

Infrastructure refers to the systems that support AI operations, including servers, storage, networks, and energy systems. Data centers are a key part of this infrastructure, providing the physical space where AI systems operate.

How These Components Work Together

AI systems function by combining all foundational components into a single process. Data is collected and analyzed using algorithms. This process creates a model that can recognize patterns and make decisions. The entire system is powered by computing machines and supported by infrastructure.

Why Understanding the Foundation Matters

Many people use AI tools without understanding how they work. This can lead to confusion, misuse, or over-reliance on technology. By understanding the foundation of AI, students and educators can:

Develop critical thinking skills

Use AI tools more responsibly

Recognize the limitations of AI systems

Build a deeper understanding of modern technology

Real-World Example

When a student asks a chatbot a question, the response does not come from "thinking" like a human. Instead, the AI system uses a trained model that has learned patterns from large amounts of data. It follows algorithms to predict the most appropriate answer, using powerful computers and infrastructure to deliver the response quickly.

This process is also influenced by how the question is asked. The words, structure, and clarity of a question—often referred to as a *prompt*—can affect the quality of the response. Learning how to communicate effectively with AI systems is an important skill known as prompt engineering. For further understanding, students and educators may explore *What to Say When You Talk to Yourself: A Guide to Prompt Engineering* by Susie Hala, which explains how carefully structured prompts can guide AI responses more effectively.

Conclusion

The foundation of Artificial Intelligence is built on data, algorithms, models, computing power, and infrastructure. These components work together to create systems that can learn, predict, and assist humans. Understanding this foundation helps students move beyond simply using AI tools and toward truly understanding how artificial intelligence works.

The Foundational Families of Artificial Intelligence

Introduction

Artificial intelligence is often described as a powerful technology, but in reality, it is not a single system. It is a combination of multiple components working together to create intelligent behavior.

To better understand how artificial intelligence works, it is helpful to break it down into organized groups. In the IntelliGloss framework, these groups are called **Foundational Families of Artificial Intelligence**.

Each family represents a key part of how AI systems are built and operate. Some families focus on how information is created and stored. Others focus on how machines learn, make decisions, process language, or perform tasks. Additional families represent the physical hardware, energy systems, and global infrastructure that make artificial intelligence possible.

When these families work together, they form a complete AI system.

This approach allows students and educators to move beyond simply using artificial intelligence tools and begin to understand what is happening behind the scenes. Instead of viewing AI as a mystery, learners can see it as a structured system made up of clearly defined components.

The diagram on the next page provides a visual overview of these families and how they connect to form the foundation of artificial intelligence.

By learning each family step by step, students develop a deeper understanding of how AI systems process information, learn from data, and interact with the world.

Understanding the Foundational Families of Artificial Intelligence is the first step toward true AI literacy.

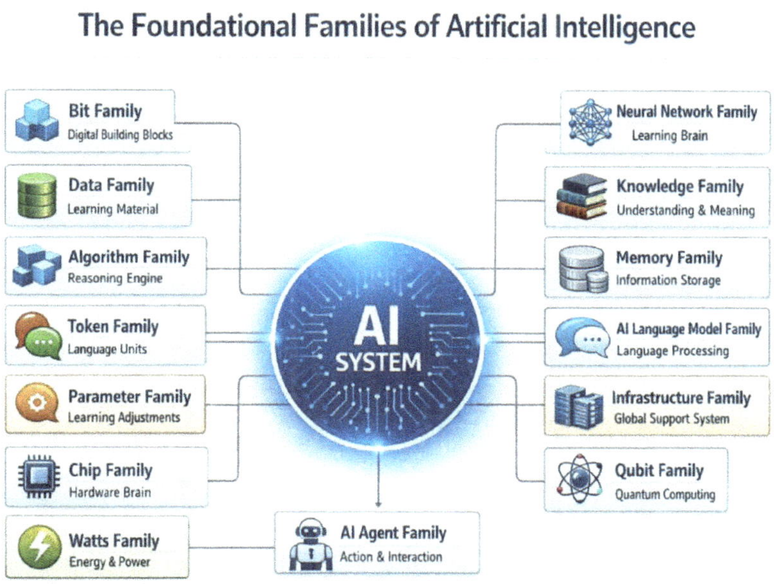

The Foundational Families of Artificial Intelligence

Family	Role	Description
Bit Family	Digital Building Blocks	The smallest unit of digital information (0 or 1). All computing systems begin with bits.
Algorithm Family	Reasoning Engine	Step-by-step instructions that tell computers how to solve problems and process information.
Token Family	Language Units	Pieces of text used by AI models to understand and generate human language.

Family	Role	Description
Parameter Family	Learning Adjustment System	Adjustable numerical values inside AI models that allow them to learn patterns from data.
Data Family	Learning Material	The information AI studies in order to learn patterns, relationships, and knowledge.
Logic Family	Decision Rules	The reasoning structures that allow AI systems to make decisions and evaluate conditions.
Memory Family	Information Storage	Systems that store and retrieve information so AI models can access past knowledge and context.
Knowledge Family	Understanding & Meaning	Structured information that allows AI to represent facts, relationships, and concepts.
Neural Network Family	Learning Brain	Interconnected layers of artificial neurons that enable AI systems to recognize patterns, learn from data, and make predictions.
AI Model Family	Intelligence Engine	The trained system that uses data, parameters, and neural networks to perform tasks such as prediction, classification, and generation.
AI Translator Architecture Family	Language Conversion System	Systems that transform input into output, enabling AI to convert text, speech, or images into meaningful responses.
AI Agent Family	Action and Task Execution System	AI systems designed to perceive information, make decisions, and carry out tasks autonomously or semi-autonomously.
Chip Family	Hardware Brain	Physical processors (GPUs, TPUs, CPUs, NPUs) that perform AI computations.
Watts Family	Energy Power	The electrical power required to run AI hardware and data centers.
AI Energy Family	Energy Source System	The total energy consumed over time to operate AI systems, including training and real-time usage.
Infrastructure Family	Global Support System	Data centers, internet networks, cloud systems, and global infrastructure that allow AI to operate and scale.
Ingredient Family	System Composition	The essential components that come together to create an AI system, including data, algorithms, models, hardware, and energy.
Qubit Family	Quantum Information Units	Quantum bits that can represent multiple states simultaneously, forming the foundation of quantum computing.

To begin understanding how artificial intelligence is built, we start with the most fundamental unit of all computing systems: the bit.

The Bit Family

Introduction

The Bit Family represents the starting point of all digital technology. Every computer system, application, and artificial intelligence model is built from bits—the smallest unit of information in computing.

A bit can hold one of two values: 0 or 1. While this may seem simple, these two values form the foundation of everything digital. When bits are combined and organized, they create larger units of data that allow computers to store text, display images, play videos, and run complex systems.

From a single bit to massive data systems, all digital information follows this same structure. This is how computers are able to represent and process the world in a form they can understand.

In artificial intelligence, bits are essential because they store the data that models learn from, process the calculations that drive decision-making, and support the systems that generate responses.

Understanding the Bit Family helps students see how simple binary signals grow into powerful technologies. It reveals that behind every advanced AI system is a foundation built from the most basic building blocks of information.

Bit Family — Visual Understanding of Data Size

How Much Data Can Each Unit Hold? (Simple Examples)

Unit	Size	Photos (Approx.)	Video (Approx. Hours)
Bit	1 bit	N/A	N/A
Byte	8 bits	1 character	N/A
Kilobyte (KB)	~1,000 bytes	Part of a paragraph	N/A
Megabyte (MB)	~1,000 KB	~1 photo	~1 minute of video
Gigabyte (GB)	~1,000 MB	~250 photos	~1–2 hours of video
Terabyte (TB)	~1,000 GB	~250,000 photos	~1,000–2,000 hours of video
Petabyte (PB)	~1,000 TB	~250 million photos	~1–2 million hours of video
Exabyte (EB)	~1,000 PB	~250 billion photos	~1–2 billion hours of video
Zettabyte (ZB)	~1,000 EB	~250 trillion photos	~1–2 trillion hours of video
Yottabyte (YB)	~1,000 ZB	~250 quadrillion photos	~1–2 quadrillion hours of video

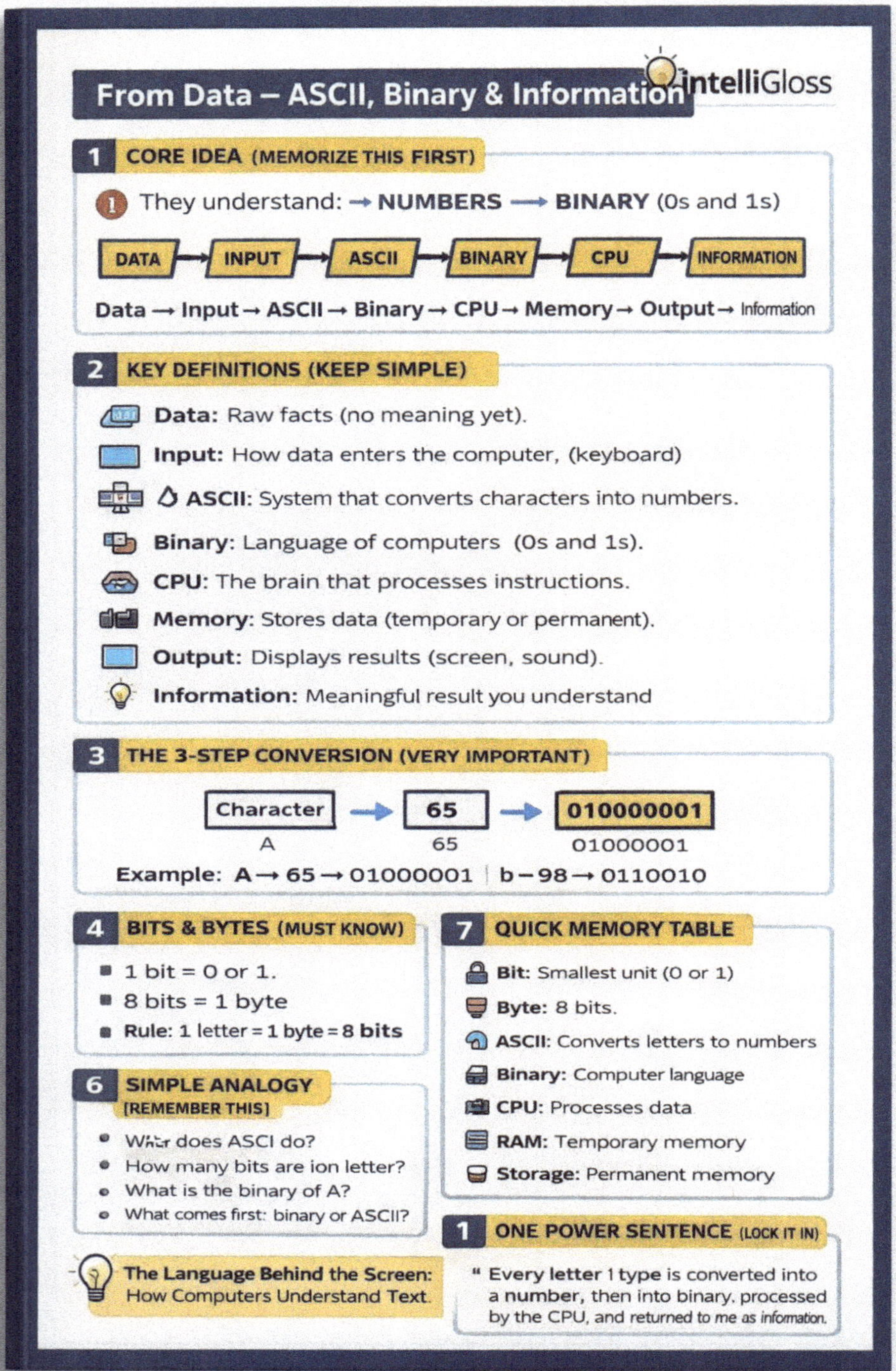
From Data – ASCII, Binary & Information
intelliGloss
1 CORE IDEA (MEMORIZE THIS FIRST)
They understand: → NUMBERS → BINARY (0s and 1s)
DATA
INPUT
ASCII
BINARY
CPU
INFORMATION
Data → Input → ASCII → Binary → CPU → Memory → Output → Information
2 KEY DEFINITIONS (KEEP SIMPLE)
Data: Raw facts (no meaning yet).
Input: How data enters the computer, (keyboard)
ASCII: System that converts characters into numbers.
Binary: Language of computers (0s and 1s).
CPU: The brain that processes instructions.
Memory: Stores data (temporary or permanent).
Output: Displays results (screen, sound).
Information: Meaningful result you understand
3 THE 3-STEP CONVERSION (VERY IMPORTANT)
Character
65
010000001
A
65
01000001
Example: A → 65 → 01000001 | b – 98 → 0110010
4 BITS & BYTES (MUST KNOW)
1 bit = 0 or 1.
8 bits = 1 byte
Rule: 1 letter = 1 byte = 8 bits
6 SIMPLE ANALOGY [REMEMBER THIS]
What does ASCI do?
How many bits are ion letter?
What is the binary of A?
What comes first: binary or ASCII?
The Language Behind the Screen: How Computers Understand Text.
7 QUICK MEMORY TABLE
Bit: Smallest unit (0 or 1)
Byte: 8 bits.
ASCII: Converts letters to numbers
Binary: Computer language
CPU: Processes data
RAM: Temporary memory
Storage: Permanent memory
1 ONE POWER SENTENCE (LOCK IT IN)
" Every letter I type is converted into a number, then into binary, processed by the CPU, and returned to me as information.

The Algorithm Family

Definition and Overview

The **Algorithm Family** represents the *thinking engine* of artificial intelligence — the set of mathematical instructions that guide how AI analyzes data, learns patterns, and makes decisions.

An **algorithm** is a sequence of steps designed to solve a problem or complete a task. In AI, algorithms tell the system *how to learn*, *how to predict*, and *how to improve* with every iteration.

In simple terms:

The Algorithm Family is the *logic of intelligence* — the invisible code that transforms data into decisions and predictions into progress.

🧠 How Algorithms Power AI

Every AI system — from simple chatbots to large-scale deep learning models — relies on algorithms as its foundation.
They determine how the model:

Processes and cleans data,

Identifies relationships between variables,

Learns from feedback, and

Improves over time.

Without algorithms, even the most powerful dataset or neural network would remain static and lifeless.

In essence, **algorithms are the teachers** that train AI how to think.

Why the Algorithm Family Matters

Algorithms are what separate automation from intelligence.
They allow machines to **reason**, **adapt**, and **learn** — not just follow commands.
For prompt engineers, understanding algorithmic behavior helps explain *why* AI sometimes misunderstands a question, repeats patterns, or changes tone after feedback.

Every AI response you receive follows an underlying process — a pattern recognition journey from input to output.

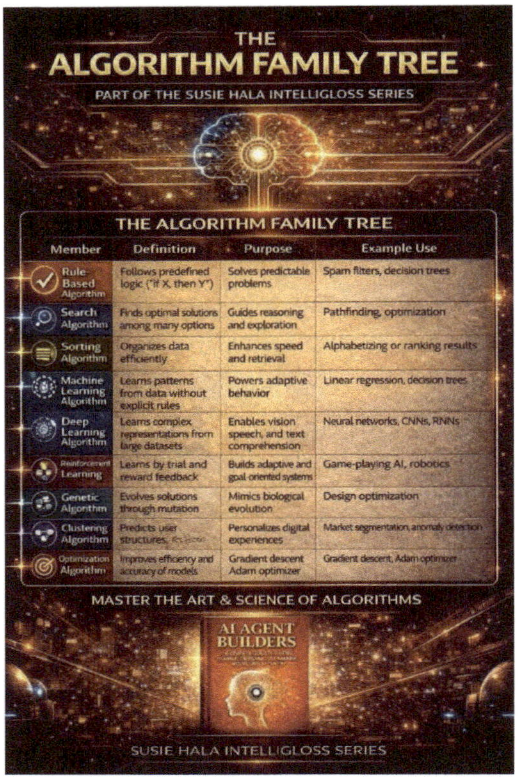

🌍 Analogy for Everyday Readers

Imagine AI as a chef in a kitchen:

The **Dataset Family** provides the ingredients.

The **Knowledge Family** gives the recipes.

The **Algorithm Family** is the *cooking process* — mixing, heating, tasting, and adjusting until the dish is perfect.

Just as cooking methods determine the quality of food, algorithms determine the quality of intelligence.

Algorithm Efficiency and Energy Use

Not all algorithms are equal.
Some are **fast but shallow**, while others are **deep but energy-intensive**.
Training large AI models requires algorithms that can handle billions of calculations per second — powered by the **Watts Family** (energy) and executed through the **Chip Family** (hardware).

The design of efficient algorithms directly affects sustainability in AI — minimizing power consumption while maximizing accuracy and speed.

Algorithms and Prompt Engineering

For prompt engineers, algorithms explain *how* the AI arrives at its answers.
When a model gives inconsistent or off-topic results, it's often due to:

Misinterpretation of input signals (input encoding),

Bias in training algorithms, or

Overfitting to certain data patterns.

Knowing this helps you craft prompts that guide the AI's decision-making — not just its output.

💬 **Quick Takeaway: The Algorithm Family is the reasoning heart of AI.**
It transforms information into understanding and enables machines to think, learn, and evolve like digital problem-solvers.

Absolutely, partner — this is a powerful section in your book because **tokens are where AI meets language**. I'll keep this aligned with your style: clear, structured, and school-district ready.

Token Family Introduction

The Token Family represents one of the most important bridges between human language and artificial intelligence. While humans communicate using words, sentences, and meaning, AI systems do not understand language in the same way. Instead, they rely on tokens—small units of text that allow machines to process, analyze, and generate language step by step.

A token can be a word, part of a word, a character, or even punctuation. When a student types a sentence into an AI system, that sentence is not read as a whole idea. It is first broken down into tokens. These tokens become the input that the AI model uses to recognize patterns, predict outcomes, and generate responses.

The Token Family works closely with several other foundational families in artificial intelligence. It connects directly with the Data Family, which provides the text used for training, and the Neural Network Family, which processes token patterns to produce intelligent outputs. It also plays a key role in the AI Translator Architecture Family, where tokens are transformed, analyzed, and reassembled into meaningful responses.

Understanding tokens helps students see what is happening behind the scenes when they interact with AI tools. Instead of viewing AI as a "magic system," they begin to understand that every response is built from sequences of tokens processed through mathematical models.

In simple terms, if language is what humans speak, tokens are what AI understands.

Token Family Breakdown Chart

Component	Role	Description	Example
Tokenization	Input Conversion	The process of breaking text into smaller units (tokens) that AI can process	"Artificial Intelligence" → "Artificial" + "Intelligence"
Tokens	Language Units	The individual pieces of text used by AI models for understanding and generation	"AI", "learn", "ing", "."
Subword Tokens	Efficiency Units	Words split into smaller parts to handle unknown or complex vocabulary	"unbelievable" → "un", "believ", "able"
Character Tokens	Fine-Grained Units	Text broken down into individual characters for detailed processing	"AI" → "A" + "I"
Vocabulary (Token Set)	Token Library	The complete set of tokens an AI model recognizes and uses	GPT models have thousands to millions of tokens
Encoding	Token Mapping	Converting tokens into numerical representations for computation	"AI" → [1234, 5678] (example IDs)
Decoding	Output Reconstruction	Converting numerical outputs back into readable text	[1234, 5678] → "AI system"
Context Window	Memory Limit	The number of tokens an AI can process at one time	Example: 8,000 tokens ≈ several pages of text
Token Embeddings	Meaning Representation	Mathematical vectors that capture relationships between tokens	"king" and "queen" have similar embeddings
Token Prediction	Language Generation	The process of predicting the next token in a sequence	"AI is" → predicts "powerful"

The Token Family reminds us that behind every intelligent response is a structured sequence of tokens working together. What feels like natural conversation to humans is, for AI, a carefully processed stream of language units transformed into meaning.

The AI Ecosystem Family

The AI Ecosystem Family is a connected group of artificial intelligence technologies, systems, behaviors, and applications that work together to help machines perform intelligent tasks. This ecosystem includes core AI systems, AI agents, agentic AI, AI autonomy, autonomous AI workers, and generative AI. Each part plays a different role in how modern AI systems think, learn, create, make decisions, solve problems, and interact with the world.

At the center of the ecosystem is artificial intelligence itself — the broad field focused on building machines and software that can perform tasks that normally require human intelligence. AI agents act as the systems that carry out goals and actions. Agentic AI describes the ability of AI systems to plan, reason, adapt, and pursue objectives with limited human guidance. AI autonomy represents the level of independence an AI system has while making decisions and taking actions. AI autonomous workers apply these capabilities to perform real-world tasks like digital employees or assistants. Generative AI adds the ability to create new content such as text, images, music, video, code, and designs.

The AI Ecosystem Family demonstrates that modern artificial intelligence is no longer just one single technology. Instead, it is an interconnected environment of systems, tools, intelligence, automation, creativity, and human collaboration. As AI continues to evolve, these technologies are becoming increasingly integrated into education, business, healthcare, communication, cybersecurity, research, and everyday life.

Understanding the AI Ecosystem Family helps students, educators, and readers see how the different parts of AI connect together to shape the future of intelligent systems and the digital world.

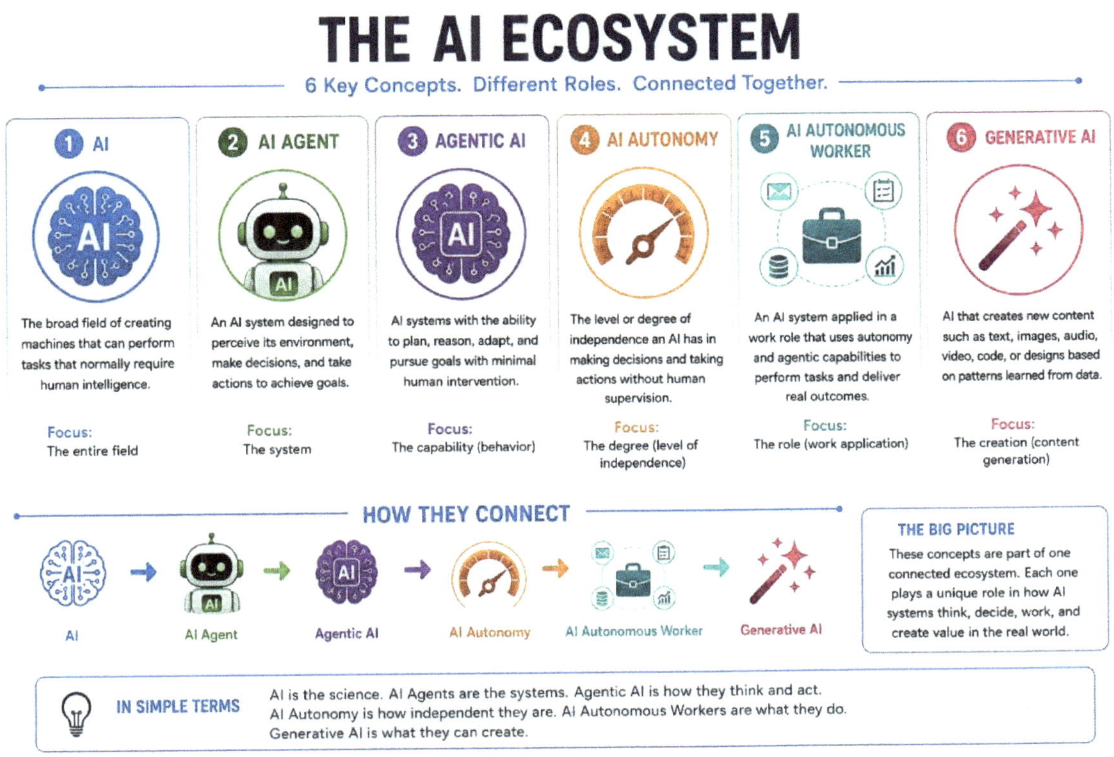

Parameter Family Introduction

The Parameter Family represents the internal learning system of artificial intelligence. While tokens provide the language and data provides the learning material, parameters are what allow AI systems to adjust, improve, and make intelligent decisions over time.

In simple terms, parameters are numerical values inside an AI model that change as the system learns. These values are not visible to users, but they play a critical role in how the model understands patterns, relationships, and meaning. Every time an AI system is trained, it adjusts its parameters to better predict outcomes and generate accurate responses.

Parameters exist throughout neural networks, where they act as the connections between artificial neurons. Each connection has a weight, which determines how important a particular piece of information is. During training, these weights are continuously adjusted based on data, allowing the system to improve its performance.

The Parameter Family works closely with the Data Family, which provides the information needed for learning, and the Neural Network Family, which organizes how parameters are structured and applied. It also supports the Token Family by helping the model interpret and predict sequences of language.

Understanding parameters helps students recognize that AI is not simply programmed with fixed rules. Instead, it learns by adjusting internal values that guide how it processes information. These adjustments are what allow AI systems to evolve from simple pattern recognition to complex reasoning and decision-making.

In essence, if data is what AI learns from, parameters are how AI learns.

Parameter Family Breakdown Chart

Component	Role	Description	Example
Parameters	Learning Values	Numerical values inside an AI model that are adjusted during training	Millions or billions of values inside a model
Weights	Connection Strength	Values that determine how strongly one neuron influences another	A higher weight = stronger influence
Bias	Adjustment Factor	A value added to help the model shift and fine-tune outputs	Helps improve accuracy in predictions
Training Process	Learning Mechanism	The process of adjusting parameters using data to improve performance	Model improves after analyzing many examples

Component	Role	Description	Example
Loss Function	Error Measurement	Measures how far the model's prediction is from the correct answer	Lower loss = better performance
Optimization Algorithm	Adjustment Strategy	Method used to update parameters efficiently	Gradient Descent adjusts weights step by step
Gradient	Direction of Change	Indicates how parameters should change to reduce error	Shows whether to increase or decrease a value
Backpropagation	Learning Process	System that sends error signals backward to update parameters	Adjusts earlier layers based on output error
Hyperparameters	Control Settings	External settings that guide how training happens (not learned)	Learning rate, batch size
Model Size	Capacity Indicator	The total number of parameters in a model	Larger models = more learning capacity

The Parameter Family is the hidden engine of learning in artificial intelligence. While users interact with outputs, it is the continuous adjustment of parameters behind the scenes that makes intelligent behavior possible.

Data Family Introduction

The Data Family represents the foundation of learning in artificial intelligence. Every AI system depends on data to develop knowledge, recognize patterns, and make decisions. Without data, artificial intelligence cannot learn, adapt, or function effectively.

Data can take many forms, including text, images, audio, video, and numerical information. These inputs provide the raw material that AI systems analyze during training. By studying large amounts of data, AI models begin to identify patterns, relationships, and structures that allow them to make predictions and generate responses.

The quality and diversity of data play a critical role in how well an AI system performs. Accurate, balanced, and relevant data helps models produce reliable results, while poor or biased data can lead to incorrect or unfair outcomes. This is why data collection, preparation, and evaluation are essential steps in the development of responsible AI systems.

The Data Family works closely with the Parameter Family, which adjusts internal values based on data, and the Neural Network Family, which processes and organizes data through layers of computation. It also supports the Token Family when dealing with language, as text data is converted into tokens for analysis.

Understanding the Data Family helps students recognize that AI does not "know" things on its own. Instead, it learns from the information it is given. The more meaningful and well-prepared the data, the more capable the AI system becomes.

In simple terms, data is the source of knowledge, and it is the starting point for all artificial intelligence.

Data Family Breakdown Chart

Component	Role	Description	Example
Data	Learning Material	Raw information used by AI systems to learn patterns and relationships	Text, images, audio, numbers
Dataset	Organized Collection	A structured group of data used for training and evaluation	A folder of labeled images
Training Data	Learning Input	Data used to teach the AI model during training	Thousands of sentences for a language model
Validation Data	Performance Check	Data used to tune the model during training without directly learning from it	Helps prevent overfitting
Test Data	Final Evaluation	Data used to measure how well the model performs after training	New unseen examples
Structured Data	Organized Format	Data arranged in tables with clear categories	Spreadsheets, databases
Unstructured Data	Flexible Format	Data without a predefined structure	Text documents, images, videos
Labeled Data	Guided Learning	Data tagged with correct answers to guide training	Image labeled "cat" or "dog"
Unlabeled Data	Self-Learning Input	Data without labels, used in unsupervised learning	Raw text without categories
Data Quality	Accuracy Measure	The reliability and correctness of data	Clean, complete, and consistent data
Data Bias	Imbalance Issue	When data does not represent all groups fairly	Skewed or incomplete datasets
Data Preprocessing	Preparation Step	Cleaning and organizing data before training	Removing errors, formatting text

The Data Family reminds us that artificial intelligence is only as strong as the information it learns from. High-quality data leads to meaningful insights, while poor data can limit or misguide intelligent systems.

Memory Family Introduction

The Memory Family represents how artificial intelligence systems store, retain, and retrieve information. Just as humans rely on memory to recall past experiences, learn new concepts, and make decisions, AI systems depend on memory to access previously processed information and maintain context.

In artificial intelligence, memory is not a single component but a collection of mechanisms that allow systems to handle information over time. Some forms of memory are short-term, holding information temporarily while a task is being completed. Other forms are long-term, storing learned knowledge that can be used across different tasks and interactions.

Memory plays a critical role in enabling AI systems to understand sequences, maintain context in conversations, and improve decision-making. For example, when a user interacts with a language model, the system uses memory to keep track of previous words, sentences, or prompts in order to generate coherent and relevant responses.

The Memory Family works closely with the Data Family, which provides the information to be stored, and the Parameter Family, which encodes learned knowledge within the model. It also supports the Neural Network Family by enabling systems to process sequences and retain important patterns over time.

Understanding the Memory Family helps students see that AI is not simply reacting to individual inputs in isolation. Instead, it relies on stored information and contextual awareness to produce meaningful and consistent outputs.

In simple terms, if data is what AI learns from, memory is how AI remembers and uses what it has learned.

Memory Family Breakdown Chart

Component	Role	Description	Example
Memory	Information Storage	The ability of an AI system to store and access information	Retaining previous inputs in a task
Short-Term Memory	Temporary Storage	Holds information for immediate processing	Keeping track of words in a sentence
Long-Term Memory	Persistent Storage	Stores learned knowledge for future use	Knowledge embedded in model parameters
Context Memory	Conversation Tracking	Maintains information within a specific interaction	Remembering earlier parts of a prompt
Working Memory	Active Processing	Handles information currently being used in computation	Processing a sequence step by step

Component	Role	Description	Example
External Memory	Extended Storage	Memory stored outside the model for retrieval	Databases, vector stores
Internal Memory	Embedded Knowledge	Information stored within the model itself	Learned patterns inside neural networks
Sequence Memory	Order Awareness	Tracks the order of inputs over time	Understanding sentence structure
Retrieval Mechanism	Access System	Retrieves stored information when needed	Searching relevant past data
Attention Mechanism	Focus System	Highlights important parts of memory for processing	Focusing on key words in a sentence
Memory Capacity	Storage Limit	The amount of information the system can handle at once	Context window size

The Memory Family shows that intelligence is not just about processing information in the moment, but about retaining, organizing, and using knowledge over time to create meaningful understanding.

Knowledge Family Introduction

The Knowledge Family represents how artificial intelligence organizes, connects, and uses information to create understanding. While data provides raw information and memory stores it, knowledge is what gives that information meaning and structure.

In artificial intelligence, knowledge is not simply a collection of facts. It is the result of identifying relationships, patterns, and connections within data. AI systems use knowledge to recognize concepts, make decisions, and generate meaningful responses. This allows machines to move beyond simple data processing and toward more intelligent behavior.

Knowledge can be represented in different ways within AI systems. Some forms are structured, such as databases and knowledge graphs, where relationships between concepts are clearly defined. Other forms are learned implicitly through neural networks, where patterns are encoded within parameters and used to guide predictions.

The Knowledge Family works closely with the Data Family, which provides the information needed to build knowledge, and the Memory Family, which stores and retrieves that information. It also connects with the Parameter Family, where learned knowledge is embedded within the model, and the Neural Network Family, which processes and organizes that knowledge.

Understanding the Knowledge Family helps students recognize that AI systems do not simply memorize information. Instead, they learn how pieces of information relate to one another, allowing them to interpret meaning, solve problems, and respond intelligently.

In simple terms, if data is information and memory stores it, knowledge is the understanding that makes it useful.

Knowledge Family Breakdown Chart

Component	Role	Description	Example
Knowledge	Understanding System	Organized information that allows AI to interpret meaning and make decisions	Recognizing relationships between concepts
Facts	Basic Information	Individual pieces of information stored within a system	"Water freezes at 0°C"
Relationships	Connection Mapping	Links between pieces of information that create meaning	"Teacher teaches student"
Knowledge Representation	Structure System	Methods used to organize and store knowledge in AI	Knowledge graphs, semantic networks
Knowledge Graph	Network Mapping	A structured representation of entities and their relationships	Google Knowledge Graph
Semantic Understanding	Meaning Interpretation	The ability to understand meaning behind words and data	Understanding synonyms and context
Inference	Reasoning Process	Drawing conclusions based on known information	If A = B and B = C, then A = C
Rules	Decision Framework	Logical guidelines used to make decisions	If temperature < 0°C → freeze
Ontology	Concept Framework	A structured system defining categories and relationships	Classification of animals
Explicit Knowledge	Direct Information	Clearly defined and stored knowledge	Rules, databases
Implicit Knowledge	Learned Patterns	Knowledge learned through experience and data	Patterns learned by neural networks
Knowledge Integration	System Coordination	Combining information from multiple sources	Merging text, images, and data

The Knowledge Family transforms information into understanding, allowing artificial intelligence to move beyond data and memory into meaningful reasoning and intelligent decision-making.

AI Model Family Introduction

The AI Model Family represents the core system within artificial intelligence that performs tasks such as prediction, classification, and content generation. It is the part of AI that users interact with, whether they are asking questions, generating images, or analyzing data.

An AI model is a trained system that has learned patterns from data. During training, the model processes large amounts of information and adjusts its internal parameters to improve accuracy. Once trained, the model can take new input and produce meaningful output based on what it has learned.

AI models can take many forms depending on their purpose. Some models are designed to recognize images, others to understand language, and others to make decisions or predictions. Large Language Models (LLMs), for example, are designed to process and generate human language by predicting sequences of tokens.

The AI Model Family works closely with the Data Family, which provides the learning material, and the Parameter Family, which stores learned patterns. It also relies on the Neural Network Family for structure and the Chip and Infrastructure Families for execution and deployment.

Understanding the AI Model Family helps students see that AI is not just a concept, but a working system that has been trained to perform specific tasks. It is the engine that transforms input into output.

In simple terms, if AI is the system, the model is the part that actually does the thinking and producing.

AI Model Family Breakdown Chart

Component	Role	Description	Example
AI Model	Core System	The trained system that performs tasks	Chatbot, image generator
Training	Learning Process	Process of teaching the model using data	Learning from datasets
Inference	Output Generation	Using the trained model to produce results	Answering a question
Model Architecture	Structural Design	Defines how the model is built	Neural networks, transformers
Parameters	Learned Values	Internal values adjusted during training	Billions of weights
Input Data	Entry Information	Data provided to the model for processing	User prompt
Output Data	Result	The response or prediction generated	AI-generated text
Model Types	Functional Categories	Different kinds of models for different tasks	Classification, generation
Fine-Tuning	Model Adjustment	Improving a model for specific tasks	Custom-trained AI

Component	Role	Description	Example
Pretrained Model	Base System	A model trained on large datasets before use	General-purpose AI
Evaluation	Performance Check	Measuring how well the model performs	Accuracy, loss metrics

The AI Model Family represents the working core of artificial intelligence, where learned patterns are transformed into meaningful actions, predictions, and responses.

Neural Network Family Introduction

The Neural Network Family represents the structural foundation of how artificial intelligence learns and processes information. Inspired by the human brain, neural networks are systems of interconnected units, often called neurons, that work together to analyze data, recognize patterns, and make decisions.

In artificial intelligence, a neural network is made up of layers. The input layer receives data, the hidden layers process that data, and the output layer produces a result. As information flows through these layers, the network applies mathematical transformations that allow it to detect patterns and relationships within the data.

Neural networks rely heavily on the Parameter Family, where weights and biases determine how strongly information flows between neurons. During training, these parameters are adjusted to improve the network's performance. The more the network learns, the better it becomes at recognizing patterns and making accurate predictions.

The Neural Network Family works closely with the Data Family, which provides the information needed for learning, and the Memory and Knowledge Families, which help store and organize learned information. It also supports the Token Family when processing language, allowing AI systems to interpret sequences of tokens in meaningful ways.

Understanding neural networks helps students see that AI is not simply following instructions. Instead, it is learning from examples and improving over time through layered processing and pattern recognition.

In simple terms, neural networks are the systems that allow AI to think, learn, and make sense of information.

Neural Network Family Breakdown Chart

Component	Role	Description	Example
Neural Network	Learning Structure	A system of interconnected neurons that processes data and learns patterns	Image recognition system
Neuron (Node)	Processing Unit	A basic unit that receives input, processes it, and passes output forward	A single calculation point
Input Layer	Data Entry Point	The first layer that receives raw data	Pixels of an image
Hidden Layers	Processing Layers	Intermediate layers that transform data and detect patterns	Feature detection layers
Output Layer	Result Generator	The final layer that produces predictions or decisions	"Cat" vs "Dog" classification
Weights	Signal Strength	Values that determine how strongly inputs influence outputs	Higher weight = stronger impact
Bias	Adjustment Value	Helps shift outputs to improve learning accuracy	Fine-tuning predictions
Activation Function	Decision Function	Determines whether a neuron should activate based on input	ReLU, Sigmoid
Forward Propagation	Data Flow	The process of passing input data through the network to produce output	Input → Hidden → Output
Backpropagation	Learning Process	Adjusts weights and biases based on error to improve performance	Correcting mistakes
Loss Function	Error Measurement	Calculates how far the output is from the correct answer	Prediction vs actual
Deep Neural Network	Advanced Structure	A network with many hidden layers for complex learning	Deep learning models

The Neural Network Family provides the structure that allows artificial intelligence to transform data into understanding, making it possible for machines to learn from experience and improve over time.

AI Translator Architecture Family Introduction

The AI Translator Architecture Family represents the system that transforms input into meaningful output in artificial intelligence. It acts as the bridge between what humans provide and what AI produces. Whether a user types a question, uploads an image, or speaks a command, this architecture is responsible for interpreting that input and generating a response.

In artificial intelligence, translation does not only mean converting one language to another. It refers to the broader process of transforming one form of information into another. For example, text can be translated into a response, speech can be converted into text, and images can be interpreted into descriptions. This transformation process is at the core of how modern AI systems function.

The AI Translator Architecture is built on multiple foundational families. It relies on the Token Family to break input into manageable units, the Neural Network Family to process patterns, and the Parameter Family to guide learning. It also uses knowledge and memory to maintain context and produce coherent results.

At the center of this architecture is the ability to encode and decode information. Encoding transforms input into a format the model can understand, while decoding converts processed information back into human-readable output. This continuous transformation allows AI systems to interact with users in a natural and meaningful way.

Understanding the AI Translator Architecture Family helps students see that AI is not simply responding randomly. Instead, it is systematically translating input into output through structured processes and learned patterns.

In simple terms, if tokens are the language pieces and neural networks are the brain, the AI Translator Architecture is the system that turns understanding into communication.

AI Translator Architecture Family Breakdown Chart

Component	Role	Description	Example
AI Translator Architecture	Transformation System	Converts input into meaningful output	Question → Answer
Input Processing	Data Intake	Receives and prepares user input for analysis	Text prompt entered by a user
Encoding	Input Conversion	Transforms input into numerical representations	Words → token IDs
Context Building	Meaning Formation	Organizes input into a structured understanding	Sentence context tracking
Sequence Processing	Order Handling	Maintains the correct order of information	Word sequence in a sentence
Attention Mechanism	Focus System	Identifies important parts of input data	Highlighting key words
Representation Layer	Feature Mapping	Converts data into internal representations for processing	Embeddings
Decoding	Output Generation	Converts processed data back into human-readable form	Token IDs → words
Output Generation	Response Creation	Produces the final answer or result	AI-generated response

Component	Role	Description	Example
Multimodal Translation	Cross-Format Processing	Translates between different types of data	Image → text description
Feedback Loop	Improvement Cycle	Uses results to refine future outputs	Model learning over time

The AI Translator Architecture Family shows that artificial intelligence is not just about understanding information, but about transforming it into meaningful communication that humans can use and interact with.

AI Architecture Family Introduction

The AI Architecture Family represents the overall design and structure of an artificial intelligence system. While individual families such as Data, Parameters, and Neural Networks explain how AI learns and processes information, the AI Architecture Family shows how all these components are organized and work together as a complete system.

In artificial intelligence, architecture refers to the blueprint that defines how data flows through a system, how components interact, and how decisions are produced. It determines how input is received, how it is processed, and how output is generated. A well-designed architecture allows AI systems to operate efficiently, scale to large problems, and produce reliable results.

AI architectures can vary depending on the type of system being built. Some are designed for image recognition, others for language processing, and others for decision-making or automation. Despite these differences, most architectures share common elements such as input layers, processing layers, memory components, and output mechanisms.

The AI Architecture Family connects all foundational families. It integrates the Data Family for input, the Token Family for language processing, the Neural Network Family for computation, the Parameter Family for learning, and the Memory and Knowledge Families for storing and organizing information. It also works closely with the AI Translator Architecture Family to transform input into meaningful output.

Understanding the AI Architecture Family helps students see the “big picture” of artificial intelligence. Instead of viewing AI as separate parts, they begin to understand it as a coordinated system where each component plays a specific role.

In simple terms, if individual families are the parts of AI, the AI Architecture Family is the blueprint that brings everything together into one working system.

AI Architecture Family Breakdown Chart

Component	Role	Description	Example
AI Architecture	System Blueprint	The overall design that defines how an AI system is structured and operates	ChatGPT system design
Input Layer	Data Entry Point	Receives raw input from users or external sources	Text prompt, image upload
Preprocessing Layer	Data Preparation	Cleans and organizes input data before processing	Tokenization, normalization
Processing Core	Computation Engine	The main system where data is analyzed and transformed	Neural networks, transformers
Parameter System	Learning Core	Stores adjustable values that guide learning and predictions	Model weights and biases
Memory System	Context Storage	Maintains and retrieves information during processing	Context window, external memory
Knowledge System	Understanding Layer	Organizes relationships and meaning within the system	Knowledge graphs, learned patterns
Decision Layer	Output Logic	Determines the final output based on processed data	Selecting the best response
Output Layer	Result Delivery	Presents results to the user in a usable format	Text, image, or audio response
Feedback Loop	Improvement System	Uses outcomes to refine future performance	Model updates and retraining
Scalability System	Expansion Capability	Allows the system to handle increasing data and complexity	Cloud-based AI systems
Integration Layer	System Connection	Connects AI with external tools and platforms	APIs, databases, applications

The AI Architecture Family reveals that artificial intelligence is not a single technology, but a coordinated system of interconnected components working together to transform data into intelligent outcomes.

TRANSFORMER ARCHITECTURE

Definition

A **Transformer Architecture** is a type of neural network design used in artificial intelligence that helps machines understand and process language (and other data) by focusing on the most important parts of the input. It allows AI systems to handle large amounts of information at once and understand relationships between words, even if they are far apart.

Key Components

1. Attention Mechanism

Helps the model focus on important words or data

Example: In a sentence, it pays more attention to key words that affect meaning **2. Self-Attention**

The model looks at all parts of the input at the same time

Understands how words relate to each other

3. Encoder

Reads and processes the input data

Turns words into meaningful numerical representations

4. Decoder

Generates the output (like a sentence or answer)

Uses what the encoder learned

5. Positional Encoding

Adds information about word order

Helps the model understand sequence (since it reads everything at once)

Benefits

Processes data **faster** than older models

Understands **context better** (even long sentences)

Can handle **large-scale data**

Powers modern AI systems

Examples

Language translation (English → Spanish)

Chatbots (like AI assistants)

Text generation

Summarization tools

Applications

Natural Language Processing (NLP)

Voice assistants

Search engines

AI writing tools

Recommendation systems

Industries

Education

Healthcare

Technology

Finance

Customer service

Challenges

Requires large amounts of data

Needs powerful computing resources

Can produce incorrect or biased outputs

Simple Explanation (Student-Friendly)

Think of a Transformer like a **smart reader**:

👉 Instead of reading one word at a time,
👉 It looks at the whole sentence at once,
👉 And decides which words matter most.

Summary

Transformer Architecture is one of the most important breakthroughs in AI. It allows machines to understand language more effectively by focusing on relationships between words. This technology is the foundation of many modern AI systems used today.

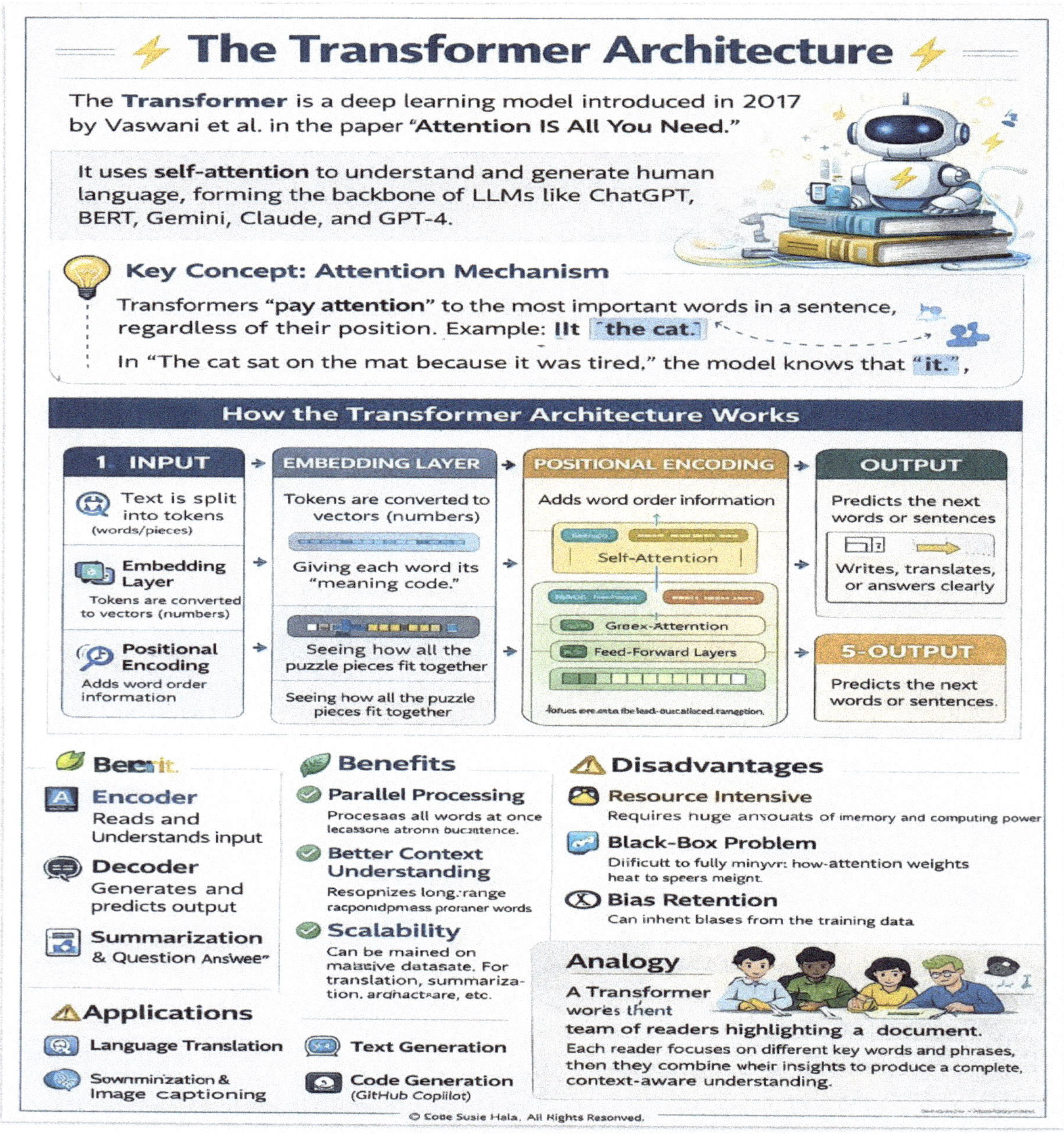

Chip Family Introduction

The Chip Family represents the physical hardware that powers artificial intelligence systems. While software components such as data, algorithms, and neural networks define how AI works, none of these systems can function without the computing chips that perform the actual calculations.

Chips are specialized electronic components designed to process information at extremely high speeds. In artificial intelligence, these chips handle the complex mathematical operations required for training models and generating outputs. Every prediction, calculation, and response produced by an AI system is executed by hardware within the Chip Family.

Different types of chips are used depending on the needs of the system. Central Processing Units (CPUs) handle general-purpose tasks, while Graphics Processing Units (GPUs) are optimized for parallel processing, making them ideal for training neural networks. More specialized chips, such as Tensor Processing Units (TPUs) and Neural Processing Units (NPUs), are designed specifically for AI workloads, enabling faster and more efficient computation.

The Chip Family works closely with the Neural Network Family, which defines the structure of computation, and the Parameter Family, which stores the values being processed. It also connects to the Infrastructure Family, where large-scale systems of chips are organized in data centers and cloud environments.

Understanding the Chip Family helps students recognize that artificial intelligence is not purely abstract. It depends on physical machines that require power, resources, and engineering to operate. These chips are the engines that bring AI models to life.

In simple terms, if AI is the intelligence, chips are the machines that make that intelligence possible.

Chip Family Breakdown Chart

Component	Role	Description	Example
Chip (Processor)	Computation Engine	Electronic hardware that performs calculations required for AI	CPU, GPU
CPU (Central Processing Unit)	General Processor	Handles a wide range of computing tasks	Running basic applications
GPU (Graphics Processing Unit)	Parallel Processor	Processes many calculations at once, ideal for AI training	Training neural networks
TPU (Tensor Processing Unit)	AI Accelerator	Specialized chip designed for machine learning tasks	Google TPU
NPU (Neural Processing Unit)	Edge AI Processor	Optimized for running AI on devices like phones	Smartphone AI features

Component	Role	Description	Example
AI Accelerator	Performance Booster	Hardware designed to speed up AI computations	Dedicated AI chips
Memory (Hardware)	Data Storage	Stores data and instructions for processing	RAM, VRAM
Parallel Processing	Speed Mechanism	Ability to perform multiple calculations simultaneously	GPUs processing thousands of operations
Throughput	Processing Capacity	Amount of data processed over time	High-performance computing systems
Latency	Response Time	Time it takes to process a request	Faster chips = lower latency
Power Consumption	Energy Usage	Amount of energy required to run the chip	High-performance GPUs use more power
Edge Devices	Local Processing	Devices that run AI locally without cloud support	Phones, smart cameras

The Chip Family reminds us that behind every intelligent system is powerful hardware performing millions or billions of calculations, turning abstract models into real-world functionality.

Watts Family Introduction

The Watts Family represents the measurement of power used by artificial intelligence systems. While the Chip Family provides the hardware that performs computations, the Watts Family explains how much energy those systems consume while operating.

A watt is a unit of power that measures the rate at which energy is used. In artificial intelligence, watts help us understand how much electricity is required to run processors, train models, and generate responses. Every time an AI system processes data, performs calculations, or produces output, it consumes power.

Different AI systems require different levels of power depending on their size and complexity. Small systems, such as those running on mobile devices, use relatively low amounts of power. In contrast, large-scale AI models operating in data centers can require significant amounts of electricity, especially during training, where billions of calculations are performed continuously.

The Watts Family works closely with the Chip Family, which determines how efficiently computations are performed, and the Infrastructure Family, where large networks of machines operate together. It also connects to the overall design of AI systems, as more efficient models can reduce power consumption while maintaining performance.

Understanding the Watts Family helps students recognize that artificial intelligence is not only about intelligence and computation, but also about energy use and resource management. As AI continues to grow, managing power efficiently becomes an important part of building responsible and sustainable systems.

In simple terms, if chips perform the work, watts measure how much power it takes to do that work.

Watts Family Breakdown Chart

Component	Role	Description	Example
Watt (W)	Power Measurement	Unit that measures the rate of energy use	A device using 100 watts
Power Consumption	Energy Usage Rate	Amount of power used during operation	AI model running on GPUs
Energy Efficiency	Performance Balance	How effectively a system uses power to perform tasks	More output with less power
High-Performance Computing	Intensive Power Use	Systems that require large amounts of power for complex tasks	AI training clusters
Idle Power	Standby Usage	Power consumed when systems are not actively processing	Servers waiting for requests
Peak Power	Maximum Usage	Highest level of power used during heavy workloads	Training large AI models
Thermal Output	Heat Generation	Heat produced as a result of power usage	Cooling systems in data centers
Cooling Systems	Temperature Control	Systems used to manage heat from high power usage	Air or liquid cooling
Power Supply	Energy Source	Provides electricity to AI systems	Electrical grid, batteries
Edge Power Usage	Local Energy Use	Power consumption on smaller devices	Smartphones, IoT devices
Data Center Power	Large-Scale Usage	Power required for large AI operations	Server farms running AI models
Sustainable Energy	Efficiency Goal	Use of renewable energy to reduce environmental impact	Solar-powered data centers

The Watts Family highlights that intelligence comes with a cost—every AI system requires power, and understanding that power is essential for building efficient and sustainable technologies.

Watts Family (AI Power Usage Scale)

Definition

The **Watts Family** represents the real-time power usage of artificial intelligence systems, measured in watts (W). It shows how much power AI systems consume at a given moment as they process data and perform computations.

Key Characteristics

Measured in real-world electrical power

Higher watt values indicate higher processing demand

Used to represent the scale of AI systems from small devices to large infrastructures

Closely connected to the Chip Family, Energy Family, and Infrastructure Family

Examples

Low watts → small devices and basic AI functions

Medium watts → computers and advanced applications

High watts → data centers and large AI systems

Summary

The **Watts Family** provides a numerical representation of how much power artificial intelligence systems use in real time, helping to illustrate the scale and intensity of AI operations.

Student Insight

Watts show how much power AI is using right now.

AI Energy Family Introduction

The AI Energy Family represents the total amount of energy consumed by artificial intelligence systems over time. While the Watts Family measures the rate at which power is used at any given moment, the Energy Family focuses on the accumulated energy required to perform tasks, run systems, and sustain operations.

In artificial intelligence, energy is used every time a model is trained, a system processes data, or a response is generated. Large-scale AI systems, especially those operating in data centers, can consume significant amounts of energy due to the continuous processing of massive datasets and complex computations.

Energy is typically measured over time using units such as kilowatt-hours (kWh), which reflect how much power has been used during a specific period. For example, running a high-performance AI system for several hours or days results in a total energy cost that goes beyond the moment-to-moment power usage measured in watts.

The AI Energy Family works closely with the Watts Family, which provides the rate of power consumption, and the Chip Family, which determines how efficiently computations are performed. It also connects to the Infrastructure Family, where large-scale systems operate continuously and require long-term energy management.

Understanding the AI Energy Family helps students recognize that artificial intelligence has real-world resource implications. It is not only about performance and speed, but also about sustainability, efficiency, and responsible use of technology.

In simple terms, if watts measure how fast energy is used, energy measures how much is used over time.

AI Energy Family Breakdown Chart

Component	Role	Description	Example
Energy	Total Consumption	The total amount of power used over a period of time	Running an AI system for hours or days
Kilowatt-hour (kWh)	Energy Measurement	Unit used to measure energy consumption over time	1 kWh = using 1,000 watts for 1 hour
Energy Usage	Consumption Tracking	Total energy required for AI operations	Training a large model
Training Energy	Learning Cost	Energy used during model training processes	Weeks of GPU usage
Inference Energy	Response Cost	Energy used when AI generates outputs	Answering a user prompt
Energy Efficiency	Optimization Goal	Reducing energy use while maintaining performance	Efficient AI models
Energy Scaling	Growth Impact	Increase in energy use as systems grow larger	Bigger models = more energy
Data Center Energy	Infrastructure Demand	Total energy used by large AI facilities	Server farms operating 24/7

Component	Role	Description	Example
Cooling Energy	Temperature Control	Energy required to cool systems and prevent overheating	Air conditioning in data centers
Renewable Energy	Sustainability Source	Use of clean energy to power AI systems	Solar, wind-powered data centers
Carbon Impact	Environmental Effect	Emissions associated with energy consumption	AI training carbon footprint
Energy Management	Resource Control	Strategies to monitor and reduce energy use	Efficient scheduling, hardware optimization

The AI Energy Family reminds us that artificial intelligence operates within the physical world, where every computation consumes energy and every system has an impact on resources and sustainability.

Energy Family (Total Power Consumption of Artificial Intelligence)

Definition

The **Energy Family** represents the total amount of electricity used by artificial intelligence systems over time. It is measured in watt-hours (Wh) or kilowatt-hours (kWh) and shows how much energy AI systems consume while running.

Key Characteristics

Measured over time (not instant like watts)

Represents total electricity consumption

Increases the longer AI systems run

Directly related to cost and energy usage

Closely connected to Watts Family, Chip Family, and Infrastructure Family

Examples

Low energy → short AI tasks or small devices

Medium energy → daily AI usage on computers

High energy → training AI models and running data centers

Summary

The **Energy Family** provides a numerical representation of the total electricity consumed by artificial intelligence systems over time, helping to illustrate the overall cost and impact of AI operations.

Student Insight

Energy shows how much total power AI has used over time.

AI Infrastructure Family Introduction

The AI Infrastructure Family represents the large-scale systems and environments that support, power, and connect artificial intelligence technologies. While individual components such as chips, data, and models explain how AI works, infrastructure explains where and how these systems operate in the real world.

AI infrastructure includes data centers, cloud platforms, networking systems, and storage environments that allow artificial intelligence to function at scale. These systems provide the computing power, data access, and connectivity needed to train models, process information, and deliver results to users around the world.

Modern AI systems rely heavily on cloud-based infrastructure, where thousands of machines work together to handle massive workloads. This allows AI to scale efficiently, making it possible to process large datasets, run complex models, and serve millions of users simultaneously. Infrastructure also ensures reliability, security, and continuous availability of AI services.

The AI Infrastructure Family works closely with the Chip Family, which provides the hardware, the Watts and Energy Families, which manage power consumption, and the Data Family, which supplies the information being processed. It also supports the AI Architecture Family by providing the environment where all system components are deployed and connected.

Understanding the AI Infrastructure Family helps students recognize that artificial intelligence is not contained within a single device. Instead, it operates across global systems that require coordination, resources, and engineering to function effectively.

In simple terms, if AI is the system and chips are the engines, infrastructure is the environment that allows everything to run at scale.

AI Infrastructure Family Breakdown Chart

Component	Role	Description	Example
AI Infrastructure	System Environment	The physical and digital systems that support AI operations	Global AI platforms
Data Center	Processing Hub	Facilities that house servers and computing equipment	Large server farms
Cloud Computing	Scalable Platform	Remote systems that provide computing resources over the internet	AWS, Azure, Google Cloud
Servers	Compute Units	Machines that process data and run AI models	Rack-mounted servers
Networking	Connectivity System	Systems that allow communication between machines	Internet, fiber networks
Storage Systems	Data Management	Systems that store large volumes of data	Databases, cloud storage
Distributed Computing	Workload Sharing	Splitting tasks across multiple machines for efficiency	Parallel processing across clusters
Edge Infrastructure	Local Processing	Running AI closer to the user or device	Smart devices, IoT systems
Load Balancing	Traffic Control	Distributes workloads to prevent overload	Managing user requests
Security Systems	Protection Layer	Safeguards data and systems from threats	Encryption, firewalls
Redundancy	Reliability System	Backup systems to ensure continuous operation	Failover servers
Scalability	Growth Capability	Ability to expand resources as demand increases	Adding more servers dynamically

The AI Infrastructure Family reveals that artificial intelligence operates on a global scale, relying on interconnected systems that provide the power, storage, and connectivity needed to support intelligent technologies.

AI Agent Family Introduction

The AI Agent Family represents systems that can take action, make decisions, and perform tasks on behalf of users or other systems. Unlike traditional AI models that only respond to input, AI agents are designed to operate with a level of autonomy, allowing them to plan, execute, and adapt to achieve specific goals.

An AI agent receives input from its environment, processes that information, and takes actions based on predefined objectives or learned behaviors. These actions can include answering questions, automating workflows, retrieving information, or interacting with other systems.

Some agents operate in simple environments, while others function in complex systems that require continuous decision-making.

AI agents often combine multiple foundational families. They use the Data Family to gather information, the Memory and Knowledge Families to retain and understand context, and the Neural Network and Parameter Families to process and learn from interactions. They also rely on the AI Architecture and Infrastructure Families to operate reliably at scale.

Modern AI agents can work independently or as part of larger systems. For example, a customer support agent can respond to inquiries automatically, while a more advanced agent can complete multi-step tasks such as scheduling, research, or system management.

Understanding the AI Agent Family helps students see that artificial intelligence is not only about generating responses, but also about taking meaningful action in real-world scenarios.

In simple terms, if AI models think and respond, AI agents act and execute.

AI Agent Family Breakdown Chart

Component	Role	Description	Example
AI Agent	Action System	An AI system that can make decisions and perform tasks	Virtual assistant
Environment	Operating Context	The space where the agent interacts and gathers information	Web, apps, databases
Input Perception	Data Intake	Receives information from the environment	User query or sensor input
Decision Engine	Action Selection	Determines what action to take based on input	Choosing a response or task
Action Execution	Task Performance	Carries out decisions in the environment	Sending an email, retrieving data
Goal System	Objective Setting	Defines what the agent is trying to achieve	Complete a task or solve a problem
Planning Module	Strategy Builder	Breaks down tasks into steps	Multi-step problem solving
Feedback Loop	Learning Cycle	Improves performance based on outcomes	Adjusting actions over time
Autonomy Level	Independence Scale	Degree of independence in decision-making	Fully automated vs assisted
Multi-Agent System	Collaboration Network	Multiple agents working together	Coordinated AI systems

Ingredient Family Introduction

The Ingredient Family represents the essential components that come together to create an artificial intelligence system. Just as a recipe requires specific ingredients to produce a final dish, AI systems rely on a combination of foundational elements working together to function effectively.

Artificial intelligence is not built from a single component. It requires data to learn from, algorithms to guide processing, models to perform tasks, hardware to execute computations, and energy to power the entire system. Each of these elements plays a critical role, and the absence of any one component would prevent the system from operating properly.

The Ingredient Family provides a simplified way for students to understand AI as a system made up of interconnected parts. Instead of viewing AI as complex or mysterious, learners can begin to see it as something constructed from identifiable and understandable components.

This family connects directly with all other foundational families, including Data, Algorithm, Neural Network, Parameter, Chip, and Energy Families. It serves as an overview that brings these elements together into a unified perspective.

Understanding the Ingredient Family helps students recognize that artificial intelligence is built, not magical. It is the result of carefully combining the right components in the right way.

In simple terms, if AI is the final product, the Ingredient Family represents everything needed to build it.

Ingredient Family Breakdown Chart

Component	Role	Description	Example
Data	Learning Input	Provides the information AI uses to learn patterns	Text, images, audio
Algorithms	Instruction Set	Guides how data is processed and decisions are made	Sorting, classification
AI Models	Execution System	Performs tasks such as prediction or generation	Language models
Neural Networks	Processing Structure	Organizes how data is processed through layers	Deep learning models
Parameters	Learning Adjustments	Fine-tune how the model learns and makes predictions	Weights and biases
Tokens	Language Units	Breaks text into smaller pieces for processing	Words or subwords
Hardware (Chips)	Computation Engine	Executes calculations required by AI systems	GPUs, CPUs

Component	Role	Description	Example
Energy	Power Source	Supplies the energy needed to run systems	Electricity usage
Infrastructure	Support System	Provides the environment for AI to operate at scale	Cloud systems, data centers
Memory	Storage System	Stores and retrieves information for processing	Context memory
Knowledge	Understanding Layer	Represents meaning and relationships within data	Knowledge graphs

The Ingredient Family shows that artificial intelligence is built from a combination of essential components, each playing a vital role in creating intelligent systems.

The Frontend and Backend Family of Artificial Intelligence

How AI Systems Connect User Interaction to Intelligent Processing

Introduction

Every artificial intelligence system operates through two essential layers: the frontend and the backend. These layers work together to transform human interaction into intelligent responses, allowing AI systems to function smoothly and effectively.

The frontend is the part of the system that users see and interact with. It includes screens, input tools, and the display of results. Whether a user is typing a question, speaking a command, or uploading an image, all interaction begins at the frontend.

Behind the scenes, the backend serves as the processing engine of the system. It receives input from the frontend, manages data, connects to the AI model, and performs the computations needed to generate a response. The backend is where the intelligence of the system operates, using models, algorithms, and infrastructure to interpret and respond to user requests.

This visual illustrates how these two layers work together as a complete system. It shows the flow of information from user input to AI processing and back to the user as a result. By understanding this structure, students can see that AI is not a single tool, but a coordinated system of layers working together.

In simple terms, the frontend is where interaction happens, and the backend is where intelligence is created.

Every AI system has two sides: what you see and what actually does the thinking.

This structure helps students understand how every interaction with AI is supported by a hidden system of processing and intelligence.

AI Qubit Family Introduction

The AI Qubit Family represents the foundation of quantum computing as it relates to artificial intelligence. While traditional computing relies on bits, which can exist as either 0 or 1, quantum computing uses qubits, which can exist in multiple states simultaneously.

A qubit is the basic unit of quantum information. Unlike classical bits, qubits can take advantage of properties such as superposition and entanglement, allowing quantum systems to process complex computations more efficiently in certain scenarios. This opens new possibilities for solving problems that are difficult or impossible for traditional computers.

In the context of artificial intelligence, qubits have the potential to accelerate learning processes, optimize large-scale systems, and improve complex simulations. Although quantum AI is still in development, it represents a future direction where computational power can expand beyond current limitations.

The AI Qubit Family connects with the Chip Family, as quantum processors are specialized hardware, and with the Algorithm Family, where new types of quantum algorithms are designed. It also relates to the Parameter and Neural Network Families, as researchers explore quantum-enhanced learning models.

Understanding the AI Qubit Family helps students see that artificial intelligence is continuously evolving. It introduces the idea that the foundations of computing themselves can change, leading to new forms of intelligence and problem-solving.

In simple terms, if bits are the foundation of today's computing, qubits represent the foundation of tomorrow's possibilities.

AI Qubit Family Breakdown Chart

Component	Role	Description	Example
Qubit	Quantum Unit	Basic unit of quantum information	Quantum bit in a quantum computer
Superposition	Multi-State Ability	Ability to exist in multiple states at once	0 and 1 simultaneously

Component	Role	Description	Example
Entanglement	Connection Property	Linking qubits so they influence each other	Paired quantum states
Quantum Gate	Operation System	Performs operations on qubits	Quantum logic gates
Quantum Circuit	Processing Structure	Sequence of quantum operations	Quantum algorithms
Quantum Processor	Hardware Engine	Specialized chip for quantum computing	Quantum computer hardware
Quantum Algorithm	Computation Method	Algorithm designed for quantum systems	Optimization problems
Quantum Speedup	Performance Advantage	Faster processing for certain problems	Complex simulations
Quantum Noise	Stability Challenge	Errors caused by environmental interference	Qubit instability
Quantum Error Correction	Stability Solution	Techniques to reduce errors in quantum systems	Fault-tolerant computing

The AI Qubit Family introduces a new frontier in computing, where the limits of traditional systems are expanded, opening the door to more powerful and advanced forms of artificial intelligence.

The AI Ecosystem Family

The AI Ecosystem Family is a connected group of artificial intelligence technologies, systems, behaviors, and applications that work together to help machines perform intelligent tasks. This ecosystem includes core AI systems, AI agents, agentic AI, AI autonomy, autonomous AI workers, and generative AI. Each part plays a different role in how modern AI systems think, learn, create, make decisions, solve problems, and interact with the world.

At the center of the ecosystem is artificial intelligence itself — the broad field focused on building machines and software that can perform tasks that normally require human intelligence. AI agents act as the systems that carry out goals and actions. Agentic AI describes the ability of AI systems to plan, reason, adapt, and pursue objectives with limited human guidance. AI autonomy represents the level of independence an AI system has while making decisions and taking actions. AI autonomous workers apply these capabilities to perform real-world tasks like digital employees or assistants. Generative AI adds the ability to create new content such as text, images, music, video, code, and designs.

The AI Ecosystem Family demonstrates that modern artificial intelligence is no longer just one single technology. Instead, it is an interconnected environment of systems, tools, intelligence, automation, creativity, and human collaboration. As AI continues to evolve, these technologies are becoming increasingly integrated into education, business, healthcare, communication, cybersecurity, research, and everyday life.

Understanding the AI Ecosystem Family helps students, educators, and readers see how the different parts of AI connect together to shape the future of intelligent systems and the digital world.

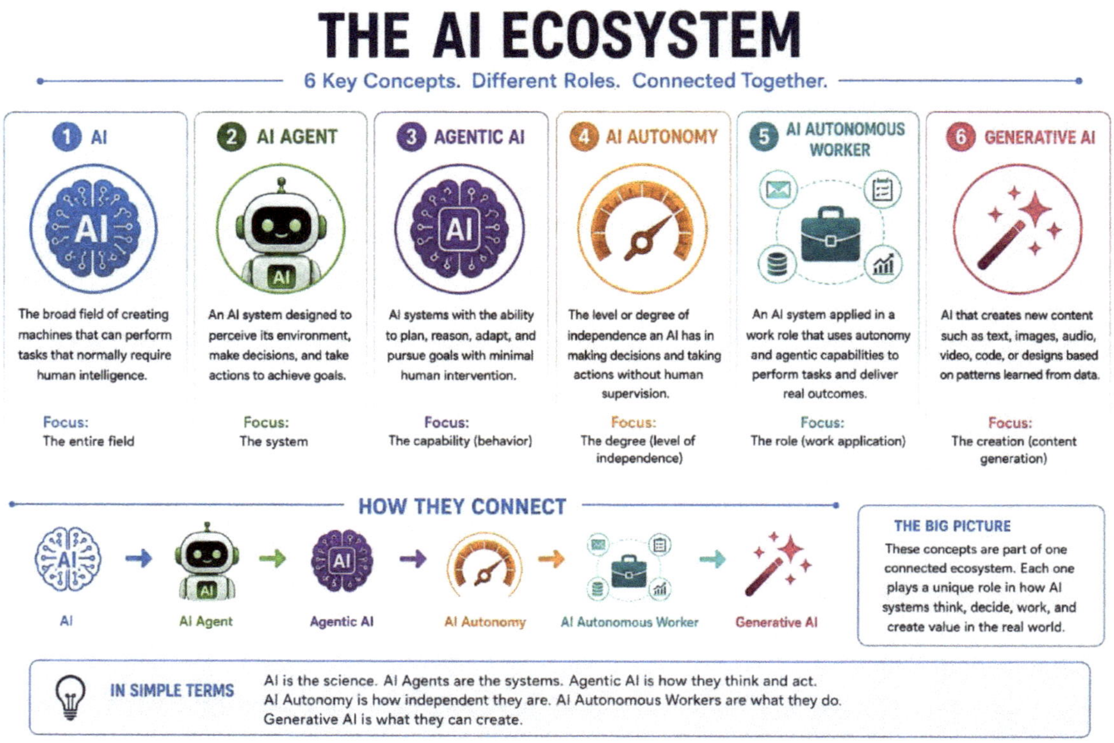

TABLE OF CONTENTS

The Ingredients of AI: What Makes Intelligence Work

The Ingredients of AI: What Makes Intelligence Work

Introduction

The Recipe of Intelligence

Artificial Intelligence, often called **AI**, is one of humanity's greatest experiments in understanding itself. For centuries, humans have tried to capture the essence of thought — how we reason, learn, decide, and dream. But just as a chef cannot create a meal without ingredients, intelligence itself cannot exist without components that give it structure, energy, and meaning. This book is a deep exploration of those components — the *ingredients* that make intelligence work in the digital age.

Imagine walking into a kitchen where knowledge is being cooked. The smell of data fills the air like freshly prepared ingredients; algorithms act as the recipe cards; neural networks are the chefs who taste, test, and adjust. The hardware and chips are the ovens that bring heat and precision, while energy provides the warmth that makes the whole system come alive. Each ingredient is essential, yet none can create intelligence alone. Just as flour, eggs, and sugar cannot make a cake by themselves, AI needs balance, timing, and the wisdom of its human creators.

In this classroom journey, students will learn how intelligence — whether human or artificial — is not magic but design. Data, algorithms, and models are not abstract words; they are living concepts that shape our world. Every smartphone assistant, translation tool, and self-driving vehicle is powered by these invisible ingredients. By studying them, we begin to see the architecture of thinking, both in machines and in ourselves.

Teachers and students alike will explore how **data becomes the foundation of learning**, how **algorithms transform data into decisions**, and how **models evolve into minds capable of adapting to new environments**. These chapters are designed to build not only knowledge but curiosity — to help readers question how far machines can go, and what remains uniquely human. Through reading, reflection, and analysis, learners will see how intelligence can be built, refined, and ethically guided.

The deeper purpose of this book is not just to describe what AI is made of, but to remind us *why it matters*. Understanding the ingredients of AI helps us design better tools, make wiser decisions, and protect our shared humanity. It prepares young thinkers to become future scientists, engineers, and responsible innovators — individuals who can use intelligence, both natural and artificial, for the good of society.

As you turn each page, you will encounter the families that make up the world of AI — the **Data Family**, the **Algorithm Family**, the **Model Family**, the **Chip Family**, the **Energy Family**, and the **Human Family**. Each family plays a role in the grand recipe of intelligence, and together they remind us that technology is not separate from humanity — it is an extension of it.

Welcome to the kitchen of intelligence.
Here, we don't just read about ideas — we *cook with them.*
We measure, mix, and taste the future.
And in doing so, we learn that intelligence — whether made of silicon or spirit — always begins with the right ingredients.

The AI Ingredient Family

Every great creation has a family of forces behind it — a circle of elements working together in harmony. In the world of Artificial Intelligence, these forces form what we call **The AI Ingredient Family**. This family doesn't live in a kitchen filled with flour, sugar, and spice, but in a digital space where logic, learning, and energy combine to create intelligence. Just as every family member plays a unique role in a household, each ingredient of AI contributes something vital to the creation of machine intelligence.

At the head of this family stands **Data**, the collector of stories. Data gathers experiences, patterns, numbers, and words from every corner of the digital world. Without data, nothing can be learned. Data represents memory — the experiences that shape what AI knows and how it behaves. Whether it's a picture of a face, a sentence in a language, or the record of weather patterns, data provides the foundation upon which all other ingredients are built.

Next comes **The Algorithm Family**, the thinkers and planners of the group. Algorithms give order to chaos. They take the raw material of data and apply rules to it, deciding what steps to take, what patterns to recognize, and what predictions to make. They are like chefs following precise recipes, knowing when to mix, when to stir, and when to pause. Every time a search engine gives you an answer or a social media app suggests a song you might like, it is the Algorithm Family at work behind the scenes.

The Model Family represents the learners and adapters — those who take what the algorithms create and continue to grow from it. Models are like apprentices who improve with every attempt. They learn from data, make adjustments, and slowly begin to make decisions independently. A language model, for instance, learns to predict words in a sentence, while a vision model learns to identify shapes and objects. In every lesson it takes, the Model Family gets smarter, faster, and more capable of understanding the world around it.

Working quietly but powerfully behind them is **The Chip Family** — the engineers and builders who make everything possible. Chips, processors, and hardware provide the environment where intelligence is shaped. Without them, even the best algorithm or model would remain only an idea. The Chip Family ensures speed, precision, and strength. They are the infrastructure of intelligence — the hands that hold the tools and keep the kitchen running.

Supporting this entire process is **The Energy Family**, the unseen lifeline that fuels it all. Just as heat powers an oven, energy powers computation. Every spark, every calculation, and every digital breath AI takes depends on the constant flow of electrical energy. The Energy Family reminds us that intelligence, whether human or artificial, always requires effort and power to stay alive.

And finally, there is **The Human Family** — the creators, dreamers, and ethical guides. Humans design the algorithms, feed the data, and decide how machines should think and act. Without human insight, AI would have no purpose. The Human Family gives direction and heart to artificial minds, ensuring that the creation of intelligence aligns with compassion, fairness, and shared progress.

Together, these families form a living ecosystem of creation — a community of cooperation where every part depends on the others. The Data Family gathers the raw material, the Algorithm Family shapes it, the Model Family learns from it, the Chip Family builds the structure, the Energy Family fuels the process, and the Human Family provides wisdom and care. When united, they create something remarkable — a reflection of humanity's endless curiosity and its desire to understand intelligence itself.

Chapter 1: Data – The Raw Ingredient of Learning

In every recipe, the first step begins with gathering ingredients. Without flour, there is no bread; without fruit, there is no juice. In the same way, Artificial Intelligence begins with **data** — the essential ingredient that allows machines to learn, think, and make decisions. Data is not just numbers or words stored on a computer; it is the digital reflection of our world. Every photo uploaded, every sentence typed, every heartbeat recorded by a smartwatch contributes to the vast ocean of information that AI draws from. In simple terms, data is experience in digital form.

Just as humans learn from the world around them, AI learns from the data it receives. When a child learns to recognize animals, they do so by seeing many examples — cats, dogs, and birds — until their mind begins to notice patterns. Similarly, an AI model learns by examining millions of examples of information. It studies pictures, sounds, or texts, then forms a pattern that allows it to recognize something new. For instance, if an AI sees thousands of images of apples and oranges, it begins to understand the shape, color, and texture that define each fruit. This is the first stage of learning, where data transforms from simple information into knowledge.

However, not all data is useful. Just as a chef chooses fresh ingredients and discards spoiled ones, AI engineers must clean and organize their data. This process, known as **data preprocessing**, removes errors, duplicates, and irrelevant information. It ensures that what the AI learns is accurate and reliable. When data is well-prepared, AI performs better — just like a meal tastes better when made with quality ingredients. In schools, this step can be compared to studying from trusted sources rather than rumors or incomplete notes. Quality matters more than quantity when it comes to learning.

Data also has personality. It comes in different forms — text, images, sounds, and numbers — each carrying a unique story. Text data allows AI to read and write; image data teaches it to see; audio data trains it to hear and speak. Together, these forms help AI understand the richness of human life. A single smartphone, for example, collects many types of data each day: photos from the camera, spoken words to a voice assistant, and typed messages to friends. Each type adds a layer of understanding, helping AI systems like Siri, Alexa, and Google Assistant become more natural in their responses.

But data is not only powerful; it is also sensitive. When people share personal information, such as their location, health, or emotions, that data must be protected. In the same way that a teacher guards a student's privacy, responsible AI must handle data with care. Data ethics is now one of the most important parts of AI education. Students must learn that with great access to information comes great responsibility. Every piece of data tells a human story — and those stories deserve respect and protection.

Understanding data also helps students appreciate their own digital footprint. Every click, search, or post leaves a trace that teaches AI about preferences and behavior. By learning about data in school, young readers become aware of how technology learns from them, and how they, in return, can learn from technology. This awareness builds what educators call **digital intelligence** — the ability to use, create, and manage technology wisely.

In the end, data is more than an ingredient; it is the lifeblood of intelligence. It teaches, guides, and nourishes every layer of AI. Without it, machines would remain empty shells, unable to reason or respond. As we move deeper into this book, we will see how the other ingredients — algorithms, models, chips, and energy — all depend on the foundation that data provides. Just as a recipe begins with gathering the right ingredients, intelligence begins with collecting the right information. And when humans and machines learn to handle data responsibly, they take the first step toward building a smarter, more ethical world.

Chapter 1 Summary

Data – The Raw Ingredient of Learning

Data is the foundation of Artificial Intelligence. Just as humans learn from experiences, AI systems learn from information collected from the world around them. This information can include text, images, sounds, videos, numbers, and patterns. Every time people use technology, they create data that can help machines recognize patterns and make decisions.

AI systems study data to learn how to identify objects, understand language, predict outcomes, and respond to users. However, not all data is useful. Poor-quality or incorrect data can lead to inaccurate results. Because of this, data must be cleaned, organized, and prepared before it is used in AI systems.

Data comes in many forms. Text data helps AI understand language, image data helps AI recognize objects, and audio data helps AI process speech and sound. Together, these different types of data help AI better understand the world.

The chapter also explains the importance of data ethics and privacy. Since data often represents real people and real experiences, it must be handled responsibly. Students learn that every online action creates a digital footprint and that responsible technology use is important in the modern world.

In the end, data is described as the lifeblood of intelligence because every AI system depends on it to learn, grow, and improve.

Chapter 1 Reflection

Thinking About Data and Intelligence

Data is everywhere in our daily lives. Every photo we take, every message we send, and every search we make online creates information that can be used by technology systems. Understanding data helps us become more aware of how Artificial Intelligence learns from human behavior.

This chapter reminds us that AI does not think like humans naturally. Instead, it learns from examples and experiences stored as data. Just as students learn from teachers and practice, AI learns from patterns found in information.

The chapter also encourages students to think responsibly about technology. Since data often contains personal information, people must learn to protect privacy and use technology ethically. Responsible use of data helps create safer and more trustworthy AI systems.

Most importantly, this chapter teaches that intelligence begins with learning. Whether human or artificial, learning depends on receiving accurate and meaningful information. Data is the starting point that allows intelligence to grow.

Chapter 1 Worksheet

Data – The Raw Ingredient of Learning

Part A: Vocabulary Matching

Match the term with the correct definition.

Data

AI Model

Data Preprocessing

Digital Footprint

Data Ethics

A. The information people leave behind when using technology
B. Rules and responsibilities for handling information fairly and safely
C. Organizing and cleaning information before it is used
D. Information used by AI systems to learn
E. A system trained to recognize patterns and make decisions

Part B: Multiple Choice

What is the main role of data in AI?
  a. To decorate computer systems
  b. To teach AI systems patterns and information
  c. To replace electricity
  d. To build hardware

Which type of data helps AI recognize pictures and objects?
  a. Audio data
  b. Number data
  c. Image data
  d. Text data

Why is data preprocessing important?
  a. It slows down computers
  b. It removes errors and improves data quality
  c. It deletes all information
  d. It replaces algorithms

What is a digital footprint?
  a. A shoe print
  b. A computer virus
  c. Information left behind when using digital technology
  d. A type of robot

Why is data privacy important?
  a. To protect personal information
  b. To stop all technology
  c. To increase computer size
  d. To make devices heavier

Part C: Short Answer

Explain why data is important for AI learning.

Give two examples of data people create every day.

Why should AI systems use high-quality data?

What can happen if AI learns from biased or incorrect data?

How can students protect their digital privacy?

Chapter 1 Answer Key

Data – The Raw Ingredient of Learning

Part A: Vocabulary Matching

D

E

C

A

B

Part B: Multiple Choice

b. To teach AI systems patterns and information

c. Image data

b. It removes errors and improves data quality

c. Information left behind when using digital technology

a. To protect personal information

Part C: Short Answer (Sample Answers)

Data is important because AI systems learn patterns and information from it.

Sample answers: photos, text messages, emails, online searches, videos, voice recordings.

High-quality data helps AI make accurate and reliable decisions.

AI may produce unfair, inaccurate, or biased results.

Students can protect privacy by using strong passwords, avoiding sharing personal information, and being careful online.

Chapter 2: Algorithms – The Step-by-Step Instructions of Intelligence

Every creation in the kitchen of intelligence begins with a plan. Once the ingredients are gathered, someone must decide how to mix them, how long to cook them, and in what order to combine each part. In the world of Artificial Intelligence, that plan is called an **algorithm**. An algorithm is a series of precise steps that tell a computer what to do. It is the recipe behind every intelligent system, guiding how data is processed, analyzed, and turned into meaningful results. Without algorithms, even the largest amount of data would remain silent and unorganized, waiting for direction.

In everyday life, we use algorithms more often than we realize. When you follow a math formula, solve a puzzle, or even brush your teeth in a particular order, you are using an algorithm — a sequence of actions designed to reach a specific goal. Computers follow similar logic, but on a much larger scale. For example, when an AI translates a sentence from English to Spanish, it follows step-by-step instructions that compare words, match meanings, and rebuild the sentence in another language. Each of these steps has been carefully designed by programmers and refined through experience, just as a chef improves a recipe after many tastings.

What makes algorithms so powerful is their ability to **learn and adapt**. In the past, computers could only follow fixed instructions. Today, with the help of machine learning, algorithms can study data, recognize patterns, and rewrite themselves to improve their performance. This is called a **learning algorithm** — one that grows wiser with practice. A common example is the recommendation system used by streaming services. Each time you watch a movie, the algorithm observes your choices and uses them to predict what you might like next. The more it observes, the more accurate its predictions become. Over time, the algorithm evolves, adjusting the recipe of recommendations to better suit your personal taste.

However, not all algorithms are simple or transparent. Some are so complex that even their creators find it difficult to explain exactly how they make certain decisions. These are known as **black-box algorithms**, and they raise important ethical questions. If an AI makes a medical suggestion or a hiring decision, people have the right to understand why. This is why modern AI education teaches students not just how to use algorithms but how to question them — how to look for fairness, accuracy, and accountability. A responsible algorithm should not only be efficient but also just and explainable.

In the classroom, students can think of algorithms as bridges between data and intelligence. Data provides the raw material, while algorithms transform that material into knowledge. For instance, in image recognition, the algorithm tells the computer how to scan each pixel, compare it to known patterns, and decide whether it matches a cat, a dog, or a tree. Each instruction is like a line in a musical score, and together they produce the harmony of understanding. Without these instructions, the machine would have no rhythm or direction — only noise.

Algorithms also teach us something profound about human thought. Our brains are natural algorithm designers. When we solve a problem, we unconsciously follow a set of logical steps. If we forget a step, we often fail to reach the solution. Computers mirror this process with far greater speed, but their logic is rooted in the same idea: structure leads to clarity. By studying algorithms, students are not only learning how machines think — they are learning how to improve their own reasoning skills.

The future of AI depends on how we design and refine our algorithms. As technology advances, new forms such as **genetic algorithms** and **neural algorithms** will emerge — ones that evolve, adapt, and imitate the learning process of living organisms. These intelligent instructions will become more flexible, capable of solving problems beyond human imagination. But with that power comes a responsibility to ensure that algorithms are used ethically and transparently, for the benefit of all.

Ultimately, algorithms are the invisible teachers inside every intelligent system. They instruct, correct, and improve — quietly shaping the thoughts of machines. In the next chapter, we will meet the students who learn from those instructions: the **models** that grow, reason, and adapt based on the lessons their algorithms teach. If data is the ingredient and algorithms are the recipe, then models are the finished dish — the living proof that intelligence can indeed be created from design.

Chapter 2 Summary

Algorithms – The Step-by-Step Instructions of Intelligence

Algorithms are the instructions that guide Artificial Intelligence systems. Just as a recipe gives directions for preparing a meal, algorithms provide step-by-step processes that tell computers how to solve problems, recognize patterns, and make decisions.

In everyday life, people use algorithms without realizing it. Following directions, solving math problems, or completing tasks in order all involve step-by-step thinking. AI systems use the same idea but on a much larger scale. Algorithms help machines organize data, compare information, and produce useful results.

Modern AI algorithms can also learn and improve over time. These are called learning algorithms. Instead of only following fixed instructions, they study patterns in data and adjust themselves to become more accurate. Recommendation systems used by streaming services and social media platforms are examples of learning algorithms.

The chapter also explains that some algorithms are difficult to fully understand because they are highly complex. These are sometimes called black-box algorithms. Since algorithms can influence important decisions, people must think carefully about fairness, accountability, and transparency in AI systems.

In the end, algorithms are described as the bridge between raw data and machine intelligence. They organize information and guide AI systems toward meaningful outcomes.

Chapter 2 Reflection

Understanding the Logic Behind AI

Algorithms are everywhere in modern life. They help search engines find answers, guide navigation systems, recommend videos, and even filter social media feeds. Learning about algorithms helps students understand that AI systems do not operate randomly. They follow structured instructions designed by humans.

This chapter encourages students to think about how logical thinking shapes both human and machine decision-making. When people solve problems step by step, they are using a form of algorithmic thinking. Understanding this process strengthens reasoning and problem-solving skills.

The chapter also reminds students that algorithms can affect society in powerful ways. Since AI systems may influence hiring, healthcare, education, and online information, it is important to build algorithms responsibly and fairly.

Most importantly, students learn that intelligence requires structure and direction. Algorithms give AI systems the instructions needed to transform information into knowledge and action.

Chapter 2 Worksheet

Algorithms – The Step-by-Step Instructions of Intelligence

Part A: Vocabulary Matching

Match the term with the correct definition.

Algorithm

Learning Algorithm

Black-Box Algorithm

Pattern Recognition

Transparency

A. The ability to understand how an AI system makes decisions
B. A system that improves through experience and data
C. A set of step-by-step instructions for solving a problem
D. An AI process that is difficult to fully explain or understand
E. Identifying repeated structures or relationships in information

Part B: Multiple Choice

What is the main purpose of an algorithm?
- a. To decorate computer screens
- b. To provide instructions for solving problems
- c. To replace hardware
- d. To generate electricity

Which of the following is an example of algorithmic thinking?
- a. Random guessing
- b. Following a recipe step by step
- c. Ignoring instructions
- d. Turning off a computer

What makes learning algorithms different from traditional algorithms?
- a. They never change
- b. They can improve by studying data
- c. They only work on paper
- d. They remove all data

Why are black-box algorithms a concern?
- a. They are too colorful
- b. They cannot store information
- c. Their decision-making process may be difficult to explain
- d. They only work at night

Why is transparency important in AI systems?
- a. It increases confusion

b. It helps people understand AI decisions
c. It prevents computers from working
d. It removes algorithms completely

Part C: Short Answer

Explain how algorithms help AI systems make decisions.

____
____

Give one example of an algorithm used in everyday life.

____
____

What is a learning algorithm?

____
____

Why should AI algorithms be fair and ethical?

____
____

How can understanding algorithms improve human problem-solving skills?

____
____
____

Chapter 2 Answer Key

Algorithms – The Step-by-Step Instructions of Intelligence

Part A: Vocabulary Matching

C

B

D

E

A

Part B: Multiple Choice

b. To provide instructions for solving problems

b. Following a recipe step by step

b. They can improve by studying data

c. Their decision-making process may be difficult to explain

b. It helps people understand AI decisions

Part C: Short Answer (Sample Answers)

Algorithms help AI systems process information, follow instructions, and make decisions step by step.

Sample answers: GPS navigation, online recommendations, cooking recipes, search engines.

A learning algorithm is an algorithm that improves its performance by studying data and recognizing patterns.

AI algorithms should be fair and ethical to avoid bias and harmful decisions.

Understanding algorithms helps people think logically, solve problems step by step, and organize tasks more effectively.

Chapter 3: Models – The Dish That Learns and Improves

In every kitchen, after the ingredients are gathered and the recipe is followed, there comes a moment of transformation — when the raw elements become something new. In Artificial Intelligence, this transformation happens through **models**. A model is the result of combining data and algorithms to create a system that can recognize, predict, or decide. It is not just a mathematical formula or a set of codes; it is a living process that learns from experience, grows through feedback, and adapts to new information. In simple terms, a model is the mind of AI — the place where learning comes to life.

When a teacher explains a concept and the student begins to apply it correctly, learning has occurred. The same is true for AI. The model learns by studying data, identifying relationships, and adjusting its internal structure until it understands a pattern. For instance, if we feed an AI thousands of examples of handwritten numbers, the model gradually learns to recognize each one — even if the handwriting is messy or different from the examples it has seen before. What makes this possible is the model's ability to generalize. It doesn't just memorize; it builds understanding.

Models can take many forms. One of the most common is the **neural network**, a structure inspired by the human brain. Neural networks are made up of layers of artificial "neurons" that communicate with each other. Each neuron receives information, makes a small decision, and passes it to the next layer. As the model trains on data, the strength of these connections changes — just like the way human memory strengthens through repetition. Over time, the model becomes better at making predictions, whether that means identifying objects in a photo, translating languages, or detecting fraud in online transactions.

In the classroom, students can think of models as learners who never stop studying. Every time they are exposed to new data, they refine their understanding. This process is known as **training**. During training, the model compares its predictions to the correct answers, measures the difference, and adjusts itself accordingly. The goal is to minimize mistakes — a process similar to how a student corrects errors after receiving feedback from a teacher. In both cases, progress is made not by perfection but by persistence.

But models, like students, can make mistakes. If they are trained on poor-quality data, they may learn the wrong lessons. This issue is called **bias**, and it occurs when the data represents only part of reality. For example, if an AI model is trained on images of only one type of face or accent, it might struggle to recognize others. That is why diversity and fairness are essential in model training. Teachers ensure that students are exposed to many perspectives; AI engineers must do the same for their models.

Another challenge in building models is knowing when to stop learning. A model that trains too long may memorize the data instead of understanding it — a problem known as **overfitting**. It's like a student who studies only one practice test so intensely that they fail to answer new questions on the real exam. Successful learning, both human and artificial, depends on balance — enough exposure to learn the patterns, but enough variation to remain adaptable.

The beauty of AI models is their ability to apply knowledge to new problems. Once trained, a model can use what it has learned to make predictions about situations it has never encountered before. This is the power behind speech recognition, medical diagnostics, and autonomous vehicles. When an AI car recognizes a stop sign it has never seen before, it is not recalling an image — it is applying its learned model of what a stop sign should look like. This ability to transfer understanding from one situation to another is what makes AI appear intelligent.

In the grand kitchen of intelligence, models represent the finished meal — the visible result of hidden labor. They carry the taste of data, the structure of algorithms, and the energy of computation. Yet even after the meal is served, refinement continues. Engineers test the model, measure its accuracy, and retrain it with new data, ensuring that it grows with the world around it. This cycle of learning mirrors our own journey as humans — continuous, imperfect, and filled with discovery.

As students study AI models, they are not only learning about machines but also about themselves. They are learning how knowledge is built, how feedback strengthens understanding, and how curiosity drives improvement. Models teach us that intelligence — whether silicon or human — is never finished. It is always learning, always tasting, always reaching for a better version of itself.

Chapter 3 Summary

Models – The Dish That Learns and Improves

AI models are the systems that learn from data and algorithms to make predictions, recognize patterns, and generate responses. A model is created when data and algorithms work together, allowing machines to improve through experience and training.

Just as students learn from practice and feedback, AI models learn by studying examples and adjusting their understanding over time. During training, a model compares its predictions to correct answers and improves by reducing mistakes. This process helps AI systems become more accurate and reliable.

The chapter explains that models can perform many different tasks, such as recognizing handwriting, translating languages, detecting fraud, and identifying objects in images. One common type of model is the neural network, which is inspired by the structure of the human brain.

The chapter also introduces important concepts such as bias and overfitting. Bias can occur when a model learns from incomplete or unfair data, while overfitting happens when a model memorizes information instead of learning patterns that can apply to new situations.

In the end, models are described as the visible result of learning in AI. They represent the transformation of raw information into useful intelligence capable of solving real-world problems.

Chapter 3 Reflection

Learning How Machines Learn

AI models show that learning is a process of growth, adjustment, and improvement. Like humans, machines do not become intelligent instantly. They learn through practice, examples, feedback, and correction.

This chapter helps students understand that AI models are not magical systems. They are trained using large amounts of information and mathematical processes designed by humans. The quality of a model depends heavily on the quality of the data and training it receives.

The chapter also encourages students to think critically about fairness and responsibility in AI. If models are trained using biased or incomplete information, they may produce unfair results. This reminds students that technology reflects the choices and values of the people who create it.

Most importantly, students learn that intelligence is never truly finished. Both humans and AI systems continue learning and improving over time through experience and reflection.

Chapter 3 Worksheet

Models – The Dish That Learns and Improves

Part A: Vocabulary Matching

Match the term with the correct definition.

AI Model

Training

Neural Network

Bias

Overfitting

A. A problem that occurs when a model memorizes data too closely
B. A system inspired by the structure of the human brain
C. The process of teaching an AI system using examples and data
D. Unfair or incomplete learning caused by poor-quality data
E. A system that learns patterns and makes predictions

Part B: Multiple Choice

What is the purpose of an AI model?
- a. To decorate computers
- b. To learn patterns and make decisions
- c. To replace electricity
- d. To create hardware

How does an AI model improve during training?
- a. By ignoring mistakes
- b. By comparing predictions with correct answers
- c. By turning itself off
- d. By deleting all data

Which of the following is an example of an AI model application?

a. Image recognition
b. Cooking food
c. Building furniture
d. Washing clothes

What can happen if a model learns from biased data?

a. It becomes fairer automatically
b. It may produce unfair or inaccurate results
c. It stops functioning forever
d. It creates electricity

What is overfitting?

a. Learning patterns too generally
b. Forgetting all training data
c. Memorizing training data too closely instead of learning patterns
d. Replacing algorithms with hardware

Part C: Short Answer

Explain what an AI model is.

Why is training important for AI models?

What is a neural network?

Why is high-quality data important when building AI models?

How are AI models similar to human learning?

Chapter 3 Quiz

Models – The Dish That Learns and Improves

True or False

AI models can learn patterns from data. _______

Neural networks are inspired by the human brain. _______

Bias in AI models always improves fairness. _______

Training helps AI systems improve accuracy. _______

Overfitting occurs when a model memorizes information too closely. _______

Multiple Choice

Which process teaches an AI model using examples?
- a. Cooling
- b. Training
- c. Encryption
- d. Storage

Which type of model is inspired by brain-like connections?
- a. Neural Network
- b. Firewall
- c. Database
- d. Router

What is the goal of training an AI model?
- a. To increase mistakes
- b. To improve predictions and accuracy
- c. To remove all algorithms
- d. To stop learning

Why is fairness important in AI models?
- a. To prevent bias and harmful decisions
- b. To increase confusion
- c. To slow down computers
- d. To reduce storage space

What helps AI models improve over time?
- a. Feedback and correction

b. Ignoring data
c. Turning off the system
d. Deleting all information

Chapter 3 Answer Key

Models – The Dish That Learns and Improves

Worksheet Answers

Part A: Vocabulary Matching

E

C

B

D

A

Part B: Multiple Choice

b. To learn patterns and make decisions

b. By comparing predictions with correct answers

a. Image recognition

b. It may produce unfair or inaccurate results

c. Memorizing training data too closely instead of learning patterns

Part C: Short Answer (Sample Answers)

An AI model is a system trained to recognize patterns, make predictions, or generate responses using data.

Training helps AI models improve accuracy by learning from examples and correcting mistakes.

A neural network is a brain-inspired AI system made of connected artificial neurons.

High-quality data helps models produce accurate, fair, and reliable results.

Both AI models and humans learn through practice, feedback, and experience.

Quiz Answer Key

Models – The Dish That Learns and Improves

True

True

False

True

True

b. Training

a. Neural Network

b. To improve predictions and accuracy

a. To prevent bias and harmful decisions

a. Feedback and correction

Chapter 4: Neural Networks – The Brain of Artificial Intelligence

Every intelligent being needs a brain — something that processes information, connects ideas, and produces responses. For humans, that brain is a biological marvel made of billions of neurons communicating through tiny electrical impulses. For Artificial Intelligence, the equivalent structure is known as a **neural network**. It is a system of interconnected layers of digital "neurons" designed to imitate the way the human brain learns, remembers, and reasons. Neural networks are the hidden power behind many of today's intelligent technologies — from voice recognition and image analysis to creative tools that write poetry, compose music, and generate art.

The idea of the neural network began with a simple observation: humans learn through connections. When a baby sees a dog for the first time, their brain doesn't instantly store one perfect image of a dog. Instead, it begins to build associations — between shape, sound, color, and motion. Each new example strengthens or weakens certain pathways in the brain until the concept of "dog" becomes clear. Neural networks in AI operate in a similar way. They connect layers of artificial neurons, each one responsible for recognizing small parts of a larger pattern, and together they build an understanding of the whole.

At the most basic level, a neural network contains three main types of layers: an **input layer**, which receives data; one or more **hidden layers**, where learning and processing occur; and an **output layer**, which produces the result. When data enters the network — such as an image or a sentence — it flows through these layers, and each neuron makes a small decision about what it sees. One neuron may detect edges, another may recognize colors, and another may focus on shapes or sounds. As the data travels deeper into the network, these small insights combine into a larger understanding. By the end, the network can make predictions, classifications, or creative responses.

What makes neural networks truly intelligent is their ability to adjust themselves. During training, they compare their predictions with the correct answers and measure the difference — an error known as **loss**. The network then uses that information to change the strength of its internal connections, a process called **backpropagation**. Over time, this self-correction allows it to make more accurate decisions. It is a digital reflection of human learning: we make mistakes, recognize them, and try again until we improve. Neural networks show that intelligence, whether biological or artificial, grows through feedback and correction.

These networks come in many specialized forms, each built for a specific task. **Convolutional Neural Networks (CNNs)** are skilled at recognizing images and patterns, making them useful in medical imaging, facial recognition, and autonomous driving. **Recurrent Neural Networks (RNNs)** handle sequences, allowing machines to understand speech, music, and text that unfolds over time. Newer models, such as **Transformers**, can analyze language with astonishing fluency, generating essays, stories, and even conversations that feel deeply human. Each architecture represents a new level of understanding — a deeper layer in the evolving mind of AI.

In the classroom, students can think of neural networks as digital learners. They practice repeatedly, make adjustments, and grow more confident with time. Like students, they improve with clear examples, structured lessons, and diverse experiences. If they are taught with poor or biased data, their learning becomes distorted. But when they are trained on balanced and truthful information, their understanding becomes strong, fair, and creative. This mirrors human education — reminding us that the quality of learning always depends on the quality of teaching.

Neural networks also teach us humility. Even though they can achieve remarkable results, they do not "understand" in the emotional or conscious sense that humans do. They recognize patterns but do not feel meaning. When a neural network composes a melody, it does not experience joy; when it analyzes a medical image, it does not feel concern. It performs its task through logic, not empathy. This difference is what keeps humanity at the heart of AI development. It is a reminder that intelligence without compassion remains incomplete.

As AI technology advances, neural networks will continue to grow in complexity and capability. They will help us solve scientific mysteries, translate ancient languages, and design sustainable solutions for our planet. But their success will always depend on the same simple principle that governs all learning — connection. Every neuron, whether biological or artificial, must connect with others to create meaning. Just as our own thoughts form through relationships, so too does machine intelligence evolve through its web of digital connections.

Neural networks are more than circuits of code — they are a symbol of humanity's desire to understand itself. By studying how machines learn, students glimpse the delicate balance between memory, adaptation, and creativity. And by understanding how these artificial brains work, they become better equipped to imagine the next generation of intelligent systems — ones guided not only by power and precision, but by wisdom and empathy.

Chapter 4 Summary

Neural Networks – The Brain of Artificial Intelligence

Neural networks are one of the most important technologies in Artificial Intelligence. They are designed to imitate the way the human brain learns by using connected layers of artificial neurons that process information together. These systems help AI recognize patterns, make predictions, and solve complex problems.

A neural network contains three main parts: the input layer, hidden layers, and output layer. The input layer receives information, the hidden layers process and analyze it, and the output layer produces the final result. As information moves through the network, each artificial neuron performs a small task that contributes to the overall understanding of the system.

Neural networks improve through training and feedback. During training, the network compares its predictions to the correct answers and adjusts its internal connections to reduce errors. This learning process helps the system become more accurate over time.

The chapter explains different types of neural networks, including Convolutional Neural Networks (CNNs), which are useful for image recognition, and Recurrent Neural Networks (RNNs), which help process sequences such as speech and text. Modern AI systems, including language models and voice assistants, rely heavily on neural network technology.

The chapter also reminds students that neural networks do not truly think or feel emotions like humans. They recognize patterns through mathematics and data, while human intelligence includes emotions, empathy, and moral understanding.

In the end, neural networks are described as the digital brain behind many intelligent technologies, helping machines learn, adapt, and improve through experience.

Chapter 4 Reflection

Understanding the Digital Brain

Neural networks show how humans have tried to model machine learning after the human brain. By studying how neurons connect and communicate, scientists created systems that allow machines to recognize patterns and improve through practice.

This chapter teaches students that intelligence is built through connections and learning. Just as humans learn through experience and repetition, neural networks strengthen their internal pathways through training and feedback.

The chapter also encourages students to think carefully about the difference between human intelligence and artificial intelligence. Machines may recognize patterns quickly, but they do not experience emotions, compassion, or human consciousness. This reminds students that human wisdom and ethics remain essential in guiding AI technology.

Most importantly, students learn that neural networks are not magical systems. They are carefully designed technologies created by humans to solve problems, process information, and improve decision-making in many areas of life.

Chapter 4 Worksheet

Neural Networks – The Brain of Artificial Intelligence

Part A: Vocabulary Matching

Match the term with the correct definition.

Neural Network

Input Layer

Hidden Layer

Output Layer

Backpropagation

A. The final result produced by the network
B. A system inspired by the human brain that learns patterns
C. The process of correcting errors and adjusting connections
D. The part of the network where processing and learning occur
E. The section where information first enters the system

Part B: Multiple Choice

What is the main purpose of a neural network?

a. To wash dishes
b. To process information and recognize patterns
c. To create electricity
d. To build furniture

Which layer receives information first in a neural network?

a. Hidden Layer
b. Output Layer
c. Input Layer
d. Cooling Layer

What happens during training in a neural network?

a. The system ignores all information
b. The network adjusts itself to improve accuracy
c. The computer shuts down
d. The hardware disappears

Which type of neural network is commonly used for image recognition?

a. CNN
b. Firewall
c. Spreadsheet
d. Browser

Why are neural networks compared to the human brain?

a. They contain human emotions
b. They use connected structures to process information
c. They replace human intelligence completely
d. They are made of biological cells

Part C: Short Answer

Explain what a neural network is.

____

____

What is the role of hidden layers in a neural network?

____

____

Why is training important in neural networks?

____

____

Give one example of how neural networks are used in everyday life.

____

____

What is one major difference between human intelligence and neural networks?

____

____

____

Chapter 4 Quiz

Neural Networks – The Brain of Artificial Intelligence

True or False

Neural networks are inspired by the structure of the human brain. _______

The output layer receives information first. _______

Neural networks improve through training and feedback. _______

CNNs are commonly used for image recognition. _______

Neural networks experience human emotions and consciousness. _______

Multiple Choice

Which layer receives incoming information?
- a. Output Layer
- b. Input Layer
- c. Hidden Layer
- d. Cooling Layer

What is the purpose of hidden layers?
- a. To process and analyze information
- b. To store food recipes
- c. To turn off computers
- d. To create internet cables

What process helps neural networks reduce mistakes during training?
- a. Encryption
- b. Backpropagation
- c. Deletion
- d. Compression

Which neural network type is often used for speech and language sequences?

a. RNN
b. CPU
c. GPU
d. Firewall

Why are neural networks important in AI?

a. They help machines learn patterns and improve performance
b. They replace all humans
c. They eliminate electricity usage
d. They stop computers from processing information

Chapter 4 Answer Key

Neural Networks – The Brain of Artificial Intelligence

Worksheet Answers

Part A: Vocabulary Matching

B

E

D

A

C

Part B: Multiple Choice

b. To process information and recognize patterns

c. Input Layer

b. The network adjusts itself to improve accuracy

a. CNN

b. They use connected structures to process information

Part C: Short Answer (Sample Answers)

A neural network is a brain-inspired AI system that learns patterns from data.

Hidden layers process information and help the network recognize patterns.

Training helps neural networks improve accuracy by learning from mistakes.

Sample answers: facial recognition, voice assistants, image searches, self-driving cars.

Humans experience emotions and consciousness, while neural networks process patterns using mathematics and data.

Quiz Answer Key

Neural Networks – The Brain of Artificial Intelligence

True

False

True

True

False

b. Input Layer

a. To process and analyze information

b. Backpropagation

a. RNN

a. They help machines learn patterns and improve performance

Chapter 5 : Chips and Hardware – The Kitchen Tools of Intelligence

In every great kitchen, even the most skilled chef is only as good as the tools they use. A sharp knife, a sturdy pan, and a reliable oven turn raw ingredients into a masterpiece. In the world of Artificial Intelligence, these tools are the **chips and hardware** — the physical foundation that allows data, algorithms, and models to come alive. They are the hands and muscles of AI, transforming abstract ideas into real computations, fast responses, and intelligent actions. Without them, the most brilliant software would remain silent — like a recipe with no stove to cook it on.

The story of AI hardware begins deep inside a small piece of silicon called a **chip**. Within that tiny space are millions, sometimes billions, of microscopic circuits that carry electrical signals — the lifeblood of all digital thinking. These chips are designed to perform calculations at extraordinary speed, breaking down complex problems into smaller parts and solving them in parallel. This ability to process many tasks at once is what allows AI systems to analyze images, translate languages, and make decisions in real time. Each chip is like a team of miniature workers, each performing a small task that contributes to a much larger result.

There are several types of chips that play different roles in the AI kitchen. The **CPU**, or Central Processing Unit, is often described as the general-purpose worker — flexible and precise, capable of handling a wide range of tasks. It has powered computers for decades and remains essential for logic, control, and coordination. However, as AI grew more complex, new kinds of chips were developed to handle the intense demands of learning and computation. Among them are **GPUs**, or Graphics Processing Units, originally designed for rendering images in video games but later discovered to be remarkably efficient at training neural networks. A GPU can process thousands of pieces of data at once, making it the perfect tool for modern AI.

Beyond CPUs and GPUs, there are even more specialized chips like **TPUs (Tensor Processing Units)** created by Google, **NPUs (Neural Processing Units)** found in smartphones, and **DPUs (Data Processing Units)** such as NVIDIA's BlueField line that manage data flow in large data centers. Each of these chips is built for a specific kind of work — some for vision, some for memory, others for speed or energy efficiency. Together, they form the invisible machinery that powers intelligent systems, from personal assistants in phones to supercomputers analyzing weather or curing diseases. In this sense, the chips are the tools of creation — the instruments that make the ingredients of AI usable and alive.

The importance of hardware extends beyond speed. It determines how accessible intelligence can be. In the early days, AI was limited to massive laboratories filled with expensive machines. Today, thanks to advances in hardware, powerful AI can fit inside a laptop, a robot, or even a small wearable device. A student with a smartphone now holds more computing power than entire universities once did. This democratization of hardware has changed the world of learning, giving every young person a chance to study, experiment, and even build their own AI systems from anywhere.

Just like tools in a real kitchen, AI hardware also requires care and energy. Every calculation, every spark of intelligence, consumes electricity. The heat produced by these computations must be managed carefully through cooling systems. Large AI facilities, called **data centers**, are built with advanced cooling and energy recovery methods to prevent overheating and waste. This is a reminder that intelligence — whether in a brain or a machine — always has a physical cost. The more we use AI, the more we must think about sustainability and the balance between technological progress and environmental care.

In a classroom setting, students can imagine chips as the quiet workers who never rest. They don't speak or think on their own, yet they make everything else possible. A single chip processes the text you type, the image you draw, or the video you record. In AI, chips allow models to train for days or weeks, running millions of tiny calculations per second. Every pixel analyzed, every sentence predicted, and every sound recognized travels through these microscopic highways of electrons. This invisible labor is the heartbeat of intelligence.

As technology evolves, the future of chips is moving toward even more advanced designs — quantum processors, neuromorphic chips that mimic brain activity, and optical processors that use light instead of electricity. Each of these innovations brings us closer to machines that can think faster, use less energy, and understand the world in new ways. But no matter how powerful these chips become, they remain the tools of the human imagination — instruments shaped by our desire to make intelligence both possible and purposeful.

The story of chips and hardware teaches students one of the most important lessons about AI: intelligence does not exist in isolation. It requires structure, energy, and design. It is built by hands — both human and machine — working together to transform thought into action. Just as a kitchen comes alive when its tools are used with skill and care, AI comes to life when hardware and humanity work in harmony. The chef and the chip share the same mission — to create something that nourishes the mind and improves the world.

Chapter 5 Summary

Chips and Hardware – The Kitchen Tools of Intelligence

Chips and hardware are the physical tools that make Artificial Intelligence possible. Just as kitchen tools help chefs prepare meals, hardware components help AI systems process information, run algorithms, and perform intelligent tasks. Without hardware, AI systems could not function.

At the center of AI hardware are chips made from silicon. These chips contain millions or billions of tiny circuits that carry electrical signals and perform calculations at incredible speeds. Different types of chips are designed for different tasks. CPUs handle general-purpose operations, while GPUs are especially useful for processing large amounts of data needed for AI and neural networks.

The chapter also introduces specialized chips such as TPUs, NPUs, and DPUs, which are built for specific AI functions like machine learning, mobile devices, and data processing. Together, these technologies form the infrastructure that powers modern AI systems.

Hardware has also made AI more accessible. In the past, advanced computing systems were limited to large research centers. Today, powerful AI technology can fit inside smartphones, laptops, and wearable devices, allowing more people to learn and experiment with AI.

The chapter explains that hardware requires energy and cooling systems to operate efficiently. AI systems consume electricity and produce heat, which means engineers must carefully manage power and sustainability.

In the end, chips and hardware are described as the physical foundation of AI — the tools that transform ideas and algorithms into real-world intelligence.

Chapter 5 Reflection

Understanding the Physical Side of Intelligence

When people think about Artificial Intelligence, they often focus on software, algorithms, or data. However, this chapter reminds students that intelligence also depends on physical tools and infrastructure. AI cannot exist without hardware that processes information and powers computation.

The chapter encourages students to think about how technology has evolved over time. Small devices today contain more computing power than entire buildings once held decades ago. This shows how human innovation continues to make technology faster, smaller, and more accessible.

Students also learn that hardware comes with responsibilities. Powerful AI systems require energy, cooling, and resources. As AI grows, society must think carefully about sustainability and environmental impact. Technology should not only become smarter but also more energy efficient and responsible.

Most importantly, this chapter teaches that intelligence is not only digital — it also depends on physical systems designed and built by human creativity and engineering.

Chapter 5 Worksheet

Chips and Hardware – The Kitchen Tools of Intelligence

Part A: Vocabulary Matching

Match the term with the correct definition.

CPU

GPU

TPU

Hardware

Data Center

A. A facility that stores and manages large computing systems
B. The physical components of a computer system
C. A chip designed for general-purpose computing tasks
D. A chip specialized for machine learning and AI tasks
E. A processor designed to handle many calculations at once for graphics and AI

Part B: Multiple Choice

What is the main role of hardware in AI systems?
- a. To replace algorithms
- b. To physically process and run computations
- c. To eliminate data
- d. To create emotions

Which chip is commonly used to train neural networks efficiently?
- a. GPU
- b. Keyboard
- c. Speaker
- d. Microphone

Why are GPUs useful for AI?
- a. They can process many tasks at the same time
- b. They store food recipes
- c. They remove electricity from systems
- d. They replace all CPUs completely

What problem is created when AI systems consume large amounts of power?
- a. They become invisible
- b. They produce heat and require cooling
- c. They stop using data
- d. They lose all algorithms

Why has modern hardware made AI more accessible?
- a. AI can now run on smaller and more affordable devices
- b. Computers no longer use electricity
- c. Hardware no longer needs chips
- d. AI systems only exist in laboratories

Part C: Short Answer

Explain the role of chips in Artificial Intelligence.

What is the difference between a CPU and a GPU?

Why are data centers important for AI systems?

Why do AI systems require cooling systems?

How has modern hardware changed education and technology access?

Chapter 5 Quiz

Chips and Hardware – The Kitchen Tools of Intelligence

True or False

Hardware is the physical foundation of AI systems. _______

GPUs are useful for processing many calculations at once. _______

AI systems do not require electricity to function. _______

Data centers help store and manage large AI systems. _______

Modern hardware has made AI less accessible to students. _______

Multiple Choice

What does CPU stand for?
a. Central Processing Unit

b. Computer Power Utility
c. Core Programming Unit
d. Central Program Utility

Which processor is commonly used for graphics and AI training?
a. GPU
b. Keyboard
c. Mouse
d. Router

Why do AI systems produce heat?
a. Because computations require electrical power
b. Because they contain fire
c. Because they stop using algorithms
d. Because they remove energy

What is one benefit of smaller modern hardware?
a. AI technology becomes more portable and accessible
b. Computers no longer need chips
c. All hardware becomes free
d. Devices stop processing information

Why is sustainability important in AI hardware development?
a. To reduce unnecessary energy use and environmental impact
b. To eliminate all technology
c. To remove data permanently
d. To stop innovation

Chapter 5 Answer Key

Chips and Hardware – The Kitchen Tools of Intelligence

Worksheet Answers

Part A: Vocabulary Matching

C

E

D

B

A

Part B: Multiple Choice

b. To physically process and run computations

a. GPU

a. They can process many tasks at the same time

b. They produce heat and require cooling

a. AI can now run on smaller and more affordable devices

Part C: Short Answer (Sample Answers)

Chips process information and perform the calculations needed for AI systems to function.

CPUs handle general-purpose tasks, while GPUs process many calculations at once and are better for AI training.

Data centers store and manage large computing systems that power AI applications.

AI systems produce heat during computation and need cooling systems to prevent overheating.

Modern hardware has made powerful technology available on devices such as smartphones, laptops, and tablets, helping more people access AI tools.

Quiz Answer Key

Chips and Hardware – The Kitchen Tools of Intelligence

True

True

False

True

False

a. Central Processing Unit

a. GPU

a. Because computations require electrical power

a. AI technology becomes more portable and accessible

a. To reduce unnecessary energy use and environmental impact

Chapter 6: Energy and Power – The Heat That Fuels Intelligence

Every form of intelligence requires energy to come alive. The human brain uses the energy from food to think, imagine, and respond to the world. A computer, though built from silicon and metal, is no different. It too requires energy to process information, run algorithms, and give life to Artificial Intelligence. In this chapter, we explore how **energy and power** form the invisible heartbeat of AI — the constant current that allows machines to learn, react, and evolve.

When an AI system begins to work — translating a sentence, recognizing a face, or predicting the weather — it does not think magically. It performs countless electrical operations deep within its hardware. Each operation, no matter how small, requires power. Inside data centers around the world, thousands of processors hum with activity, drawing electricity to train large models that simulate human reasoning. This invisible electricity becomes the "heat" of intelligence — the power that transforms code into consciousness-like behavior. Without it, the brightest algorithm or the most sophisticated neural network would remain frozen, lifeless, and silent.

Energy in AI is more than just electricity; it represents the rhythm of creation. Every flicker of power allows an AI system to take a step in its learning journey. When data flows through chips, it sparks countless micro-reactions — tiny pulses of energy traveling through circuits at nearly the speed of light. These movements generate not only computation but also warmth. The more advanced the task, the more energy is required, and the hotter the system becomes. For this reason, modern AI laboratories use complex cooling systems, from fans and liquid coolers to massive air-conditioning networks, ensuring that intelligence does not overheat.

But energy is not infinite, and this introduces a crucial challenge for humanity. As the demand for AI grows, so does its appetite for power. Training large-scale models can consume as much electricity as entire towns. This has led scientists and engineers to develop **energy-efficient architectures** — chips and algorithms that can learn more while consuming less. Just as humans learn to work smarter, not harder, AI must learn to compute more efficiently. Green AI, a growing field, focuses on creating systems that save energy, reuse heat, and operate sustainably. This movement reminds students that intelligence, no matter how advanced, must coexist responsibly with the planet that sustains it.

In the classroom, energy becomes a bridge between physics and computer science. Students can imagine that each line of code carries a tiny spark, and when billions of sparks combine, a new form of thought emerges. Power consumption turns into a lesson in balance — too little energy, and the system cannot perform; too much, and it becomes wasteful. Learning to manage that balance teaches a deeper truth about technology and life: that every powerful mind, human or artificial, must learn to use its energy wisely.

AI's relationship with energy also reveals an important ethical dimension. The electricity that fuels machines often comes from natural resources — coal, gas, or renewable sources such as solar and wind. The choices we make about where that energy comes from shape the future of our planet. As AI continues to grow, its designers carry a shared responsibility to ensure that progress does not harm the environment. Students learning about AI today are the ones who will one day lead the charge for cleaner, smarter, and more sustainable innovation.

The future of AI will depend heavily on breakthroughs in energy. Quantum processors, for example, use quantum states to perform complex calculations using far less power. Neuromorphic chips, modeled after the human brain, operate with incredible efficiency, requiring only a fraction of the energy consumed by traditional systems. These innovations show that intelligence can evolve toward harmony — not only becoming smarter but also more mindful of its impact on the world.

Energy, then, is the unseen thread that connects every chapter of this book. It fuels the data that feeds AI, powers the chips that process it, and drives the algorithms and models that bring intelligence to life. It is the warmth that allows a cold machine to move, speak, and respond with purpose. For students and teachers, understanding energy is not just a lesson in physics or engineering — it is a lesson in responsibility, stewardship, and respect for creation.

The mind, whether human or artificial, shines brightest not when it consumes the most power, but when it uses energy with wisdom. Intelligence without balance burns out; intelligence guided by purpose lights the way forward. The same principle that keeps the stars shining also keeps AI alive — the dance of power, precision, and restraint that fuels every spark of understanding.

Chapter 6 Summary

Energy and Power – The Heat That Fuels Intelligence

Energy and power are essential for every Artificial Intelligence system. Just as the human brain requires energy from food to think and function, AI systems require electricity to process data, run algorithms, and perform intelligent tasks.

Every action performed by AI — such as recognizing images, translating language, or making predictions — depends on electrical power flowing through computer hardware and chips. These calculations happen inside processors that generate heat while operating. Because of this, cooling systems are needed to prevent AI systems from overheating.

The chapter explains that modern AI systems consume large amounts of energy, especially large models trained inside data centers. As AI technology grows, engineers and scientists are working to create more energy-efficient systems that can perform powerful computations while using less electricity.

The chapter also introduces the idea of Green AI, which focuses on building sustainable AI systems that reduce energy waste and environmental impact. Renewable energy sources such as solar and wind power may help support future AI systems responsibly.

Students also learn that energy connects AI to other subjects such as physics, engineering, and environmental science. Every intelligent system depends on balance — enough energy to function efficiently without creating unnecessary waste.

In the end, energy is described as the invisible force that brings AI systems to life. Without power, intelligence cannot operate, learn, or grow.

Chapter 6 Reflection

Understanding the Power Behind Intelligence

This chapter teaches students that Artificial Intelligence is not powered by magic. Behind every AI system is a physical process that depends on electricity, hardware, and energy management.

Students learn that technology always has a cost. Every search engine request, video recommendation, or AI-generated response requires electrical power and computing resources. As AI systems become more advanced, society must think carefully about sustainability and responsible energy use.

The chapter also encourages students to see the connection between technology and the environment. Intelligent systems can improve the world, but they must also be designed in ways that protect natural resources and reduce waste.

Most importantly, this chapter reminds students that true intelligence is not only about power and speed. It is also about balance, responsibility, and using resources wisely for the benefit of humanity and the planet.

Chapter 6 Worksheet

Energy and Power – The Heat That Fuels Intelligence

Part A: Vocabulary Matching

Match the term with the correct definition.

Energy

Power Consumption

Cooling System

Green AI

Data Center

A. Technology designed to reduce energy waste in AI systems
B. A facility that stores and operates large computing systems
C. The amount of electricity used by a system
D. A system that removes heat from computers and processors
E. The force that allows machines and systems to operate

Part B: Multiple Choice

Why do AI systems require energy?
- a. To decorate computers
- b. To process information and perform calculations
- c. To replace hardware
- d. To stop algorithms

What happens when processors perform many calculations?
- a. They disappear
- b. They generate heat
- c. They stop using electricity
- d. They become biological

Why are cooling systems important in AI hardware?
- a. They help prevent overheating
- b. They remove data permanently
- c. They replace processors
- d. They stop AI from learning

What is the goal of Green AI?
- a. To make all computers green in color
- b. To reduce environmental impact and improve energy efficiency
- c. To eliminate electricity completely
- d. To stop technological development

Which renewable energy source can help power future AI systems?
- a. Coal
- b. Wind energy
- c. Plastic
- d. Smoke

Part C: Short Answer

Explain why energy is important for AI systems.

Why do AI systems produce heat?

What is Green AI?

Why is sustainability important in AI development?

Give one example of how energy and AI are connected in everyday life.

Chapter 6 Quiz

Energy and Power – The Heat That Fuels Intelligence

True or False

AI systems require electricity to function. _______

Processors can generate heat during computation. _______

Green AI focuses on reducing energy waste. _______

Cooling systems are unnecessary in large AI systems. _______

Renewable energy may help support future AI technologies. _______

Multiple Choice

What powers AI computations?

a. Electricity
b. Water only
c. Plastic
d. Paint

Why do large AI systems need cooling systems?

a. To prevent overheating
b. To remove algorithms
c. To stop learning
d. To increase confusion

What does Green AI encourage?

a. Wasteful energy use
b. Sustainable and energy-efficient technology
c. Removing all hardware
d. Eliminating data storage

Which area is closely connected to AI energy use?

a. Environmental science
b. Cooking only
c. Painting
d. Gardening only

Why is energy considered the "heartbeat" of AI?

a. It powers all computations and intelligent activity
b. It changes computer colors
c. It removes all software
d. It prevents learning systems from functioning

Chapter 6 Answer Key

Energy and Power – The Heat That Fuels Intelligence

Worksheet Answers

Part A: Vocabulary Matching

E

C

D

A

B

Part B: Multiple Choice

b. To process information and perform calculations

b. They generate heat

a. They help prevent overheating

b. To reduce environmental impact and improve energy efficiency

b. Wind energy

Part C: Short Answer (Sample Answers)

Energy powers AI systems and allows them to process information and perform computations.

AI systems produce heat because electrical computations generate thermal energy.

Green AI focuses on building energy-efficient and environmentally responsible AI systems.

Sustainability helps reduce waste, save energy, and protect the environment as AI technology grows.

Sample answers: smartphones using AI, online searches, voice assistants, streaming recommendations.

Quiz Answer Key

Energy and Power – The Heat That Fuels Intelligence

True

True

True

False

True

a. Electricity

a. To prevent overheating

b. Sustainable and energy-efficient technology

a. Environmental science

a. It powers all computations and intelligent activity

Chapter 7: Human Knowledge – The Chef's Wisdom

Every recipe begins with a mind that understands flavor, texture, and balance. The best ingredients and finest tools mean little without the guiding hand of a skilled chef. In the same way, Artificial Intelligence depends on **human knowledge** — the wisdom, creativity, and moral sense that give machines direction. Data, algorithms, and chips may form the body of AI, but human knowledge is its soul. Without it, intelligence would exist without purpose, acting blindly without knowing why.

Human knowledge is not just information stored in memory; it is the ability to interpret, connect, and create meaning. For centuries, humanity has built this knowledge through observation, discovery, and experience. Every equation written, every story told, and every problem solved becomes part of the shared memory that shapes civilization. When we build AI, we are, in a sense, pouring a portion of that knowledge into machines. We give them data gathered from our experiments, language collected from our histories, and logic drawn from our reasoning. In doing so, we teach them to reflect fragments of what we know — but never all of who we are.

This relationship between human and machine is much like the relationship between teacher and student. The teacher provides structure, lessons, and correction, but it is the human heart that inspires curiosity and creativity. Machines can imitate reasoning, but they cannot dream or wonder. They cannot feel the joy of discovery or the moral weight of a decision. These qualities belong solely to humanity, and they are what make human knowledge the most important ingredient in the recipe of intelligence.

In the classroom, this becomes a powerful lesson for students. When they learn about AI, they must not only study how it works but also *why* it works and *who* it serves. Every algorithm written carries traces of its creator's assumptions. If the creator lacks fairness, compassion, or cultural awareness, those same flaws may appear in the machine's decisions. This is why the future of AI depends not just on technical skill but on moral intelligence — the ability to use knowledge responsibly. Teachers can encourage students to think critically about the systems they design, asking questions like: "Who benefits from this technology?" and "What could go wrong if it is misused?" These reflections turn science into wisdom.

Human knowledge also drives innovation. Every new discovery in AI — from self-learning robots to voice assistants — begins with a question asked by a human mind. Curiosity is the spark that fuels progress. Students who understand this see that learning is not just about memorizing facts; it is about imagining what could be possible. The knowledge that builds AI today is the same curiosity that led humans to explore the stars, decode DNA, and invent electricity. It is a reminder that progress is not a product of machines, but of minds that refuse to stop asking questions.

At the same time, human knowledge serves as a safeguard. It ensures that AI remains a tool, not a ruler. While machines can process information faster than any person, they cannot make moral choices. They do not understand justice, kindness, or empathy. These must come from human guidance. This is why teachers, parents, and leaders play such a vital role in shaping the next generation of AI thinkers. They must teach not only how to build intelligent systems but how to build them with care and conscience.

The collaboration between humans and machines is not a competition but a partnership. When guided by human wisdom, AI becomes a mirror that helps us see ourselves more clearly. It reflects our strengths — our creativity, logic, and desire to understand — and also our weaknesses, such as bias and error. Each reflection is a lesson in how to become wiser. The more we teach machines, the more we learn about the nature of intelligence itself.

Human knowledge is therefore both the foundation and the compass of AI. It provides direction, purpose, and meaning in a world driven by automation. Just as a chef uses instinct and experience to bring harmony to ingredients, humanity uses knowledge to bring harmony to technology. Without this wisdom, the digital kitchen would produce endless noise — powerful but aimless. With it, AI becomes something far greater: a force that extends our reach, amplifies our creativity, and helps us solve the world's most urgent problems.

In the end, the greatest ingredient in Artificial Intelligence is not code or computation but consciousness — the awareness that what we create must serve life, not replace it. Students who understand this truth become more than learners of technology; they become stewards of the future. And teachers who pass it on remind the world that even in an age of intelligent machines, it is still the human mind — thoughtful, curious, and compassionate — that remains the brightest light in the room.

Chapter 7 Summary

Human Knowledge – The Chef's Wisdom

Human knowledge is the guiding force behind Artificial Intelligence. While data, algorithms, and hardware help machines function, it is human wisdom, creativity, and decision-making that give AI purpose and direction.

Humans create AI systems by designing algorithms, collecting data, and teaching machines how to recognize patterns and solve problems. AI learns from information provided by people, but it does not truly understand emotions, morality, or human experiences. Machines can process information quickly, but they still depend on human guidance and responsibility.

The chapter explains that human knowledge is built through learning, observation, creativity, and experience. Every scientific discovery, invention, and technological advancement begins with human curiosity and imagination. AI itself exists because humans asked questions, solved problems, and explored new ideas.

Students also learn that AI reflects the values of its creators. If people design systems responsibly and ethically, AI can help improve education, healthcare, communication, and many other parts of society. However, if systems are created carelessly, they may spread bias or cause harm.

The chapter emphasizes that AI should remain a tool guided by human wisdom rather than a replacement for human thinking. Human compassion, ethics, creativity, and moral judgment remain qualities that machines cannot fully replicate.

In the end, human knowledge is described as the "chef's wisdom" behind the recipe of intelligence — the force that gives meaning, purpose, and direction to technology.

Chapter 7 Reflection

Human Wisdom and Artificial Intelligence

This chapter reminds students that Artificial Intelligence begins with human intelligence. Every AI system, no matter how advanced, was created by people who used knowledge, creativity, and problem-solving skills to design it.

Students learn that technology reflects human choices and values. AI systems are not independent moral thinkers. They rely on human guidance to ensure they are used fairly, safely, and responsibly. This makes ethics and education extremely important in the development of future technologies.

The chapter also encourages students to appreciate the unique qualities of human intelligence. Machines can process data and recognize patterns, but humans bring empathy, imagination, compassion, and moral understanding into the world. These qualities help guide technology toward positive goals.

Most importantly, this chapter teaches that learning is a lifelong process. Human knowledge continues to grow through curiosity, exploration, and collaboration. The future of AI will depend not only on machines becoming smarter, but on humans becoming wiser in how they create and use technology.

Chapter 7 Worksheet

Human Knowledge – The Chef's Wisdom

Part A: Vocabulary Matching

Match the term with the correct definition.

Human Knowledge

Creativity

Ethics

Curiosity

Innovation

A. The ability to create new ideas and solutions
B. The study of right and wrong behavior
C. A strong desire to learn and explore
D. Human understanding gained through learning and experience
E. The development of new methods, ideas, or technologies

Part B: Multiple Choice

What gives AI systems purpose and direction?
- a. Random guessing
- b. Human knowledge and guidance
- c. Electricity alone
- d. Hardware only

Which quality is unique to humans compared to AI systems?
- a. Data storage
- b. Electrical processing
- c. Empathy and moral understanding
- d. Pattern recognition only

Why is human creativity important in AI development?

a. It helps design new technologies and solve problems
b. It removes all algorithms
c. It stops computers from working
d. It eliminates electricity use

What can happen if AI systems are designed without ethical thinking?

a. They automatically become fair
b. They may produce harmful or biased results
c. They stop using data
d. They become human

Why is curiosity important for innovation?

a. It encourages people to ask questions and explore new ideas
b. It prevents learning
c. It removes creativity
d. It stops technology from advancing

Part C: Short Answer

Explain the role of human knowledge in AI development.

Why is ethics important in AI?

What are some qualities humans have that AI does not fully possess?

How does curiosity help advance technology?

Why should AI remain guided by human wisdom?

Chapter 7 Quiz

Human Knowledge – The Chef's Wisdom

True or False

AI systems are created and guided by humans. _______

Machines fully understand emotions and morality like humans. _______

Human creativity helps drive innovation in AI. _______

Ethics plays an important role in technology development. _______

Curiosity helps humans discover new ideas and solutions. _______

Multiple Choice

What is one major role of humans in AI development?
- a. Designing and guiding intelligent systems
- b. Removing all data from computers
- c. Eliminating hardware completely
- d. Stopping all innovation

Which human quality helps inspire inventions and discoveries?
- a. Curiosity
- b. Silence
- c. Confusion
- d. Inactivity

Why is ethical thinking important in AI systems?
- a. To ensure technology is used fairly and responsibly
- b. To prevent all learning
- c. To stop computer processing
- d. To eliminate creativity

Which of the following is something AI systems cannot fully replicate?
- a. Electrical processing
- b. Human empathy and moral judgment
- c. Data analysis
- d. Pattern recognition

What does this chapter teach about the future of AI?

a. Machines should completely replace humans
b. Human wisdom must continue guiding technology responsibly
c. Ethics is unnecessary in technology
d. Curiosity no longer matters

Chapter 7 Answer Key

Human Knowledge – The Chef's Wisdom

Worksheet Answers

Part A: Vocabulary Matching

D

A

B

C

E

Part B: Multiple Choice

b. Human knowledge and guidance

c. Empathy and moral understanding

a. It helps design new technologies and solve problems

b. They may produce harmful or biased results

a. It encourages people to ask questions and explore new ideas

Part C: Short Answer (Sample Answers)

Human knowledge helps design, guide, and improve AI systems.

Ethics helps ensure AI systems are fair, safe, and responsible.

Humans possess empathy, creativity, compassion, and moral judgment.

Curiosity encourages people to explore, ask questions, and invent new technologies.

Human wisdom helps ensure AI benefits society and is used responsibly.

Quiz Answer Key

Human Knowledge – The Chef's Wisdom

True

False

True

True

True

a. Designing and guiding intelligent systems

a. Curiosity

a. To ensure technology is used fairly and responsibly

b. Human empathy and moral judgment

b. Human wisdom must continue guiding technology responsibly

Chapter 8: Ethics and Responsibility – The Moral Flavor of Intelligence

Every great recipe requires balance — not just of ingredients, but of intention. Too much salt can ruin a dish, and too much sweetness can overpower it. The same is true for Artificial Intelligence. The brilliance of AI depends not only on data, algorithms, and hardware but on the values that guide its creation. These values — fairness, honesty, accountability, and compassion

— make up the **ethical foundation** of intelligence. Without them, AI risks becoming powerful but unprincipled, intelligent but unjust.

Ethics in AI is the study of how machines should behave and how humans should design them. It asks important questions: Who decides what an AI system should do? Who is responsible when it makes a mistake? How do we ensure that technology serves people rather than controls them? These questions are not just for scientists; they belong in every classroom where young minds learn about technology. They help students see that intelligence is not just about thinking — it is about choosing what is right.

Every AI system reflects the intentions of its creators. When programmers write algorithms or train models, their choices — consciously or unconsciously — become part of the machine's logic. If they use incomplete or biased data, the AI may make unfair decisions. For example, an AI hiring system that learns from past human behavior might favor certain groups over others, repeating old inequalities. This shows that bias is not just a technical problem; it is a moral one. Students learning about AI must understand that technology inherits the values of its makers, and that ethical awareness is as essential as programming skill.

Responsibility in AI extends beyond design. It includes how we use technology in everyday life. Social media algorithms, for instance, can shape opinions, influence elections, and affect mental health. Facial recognition tools can help catch criminals but also risk invading privacy if used carelessly. Self-driving cars can reduce accidents but raise questions about accountability in case of failure. Each of these examples reminds us that intelligence without responsibility can become dangerous. The goal of AI education is not only to teach how to build systems but how to guide them wisely.

Teachers play a vital role in helping students explore these ideas. Through discussion and reflection, students can examine real-world ethical dilemmas. Should an AI be allowed to make life-and-death decisions in hospitals? Should data collected from children ever be used for advertising? By engaging with such questions, students learn that ethics is not a set of rules but a way of thinking — a habit of examining the consequences of every action. This practice turns technical learning into moral education.

Ethical AI also includes transparency — the idea that systems should be explainable and understandable. People have the right to know why an AI made a decision that affects them. This is called **accountability**, and it is one of the pillars of responsible technology. Just as a student must show their work in solving a problem, AI should be able to show how it reached its conclusions. Transparency builds trust, and trust builds acceptance. Without it, even the most advanced intelligence loses credibility.

The concept of **beneficence**, meaning "doing good," is another moral ingredient. AI should be designed to benefit humanity — to improve education, healthcare, and the environment — not to harm or exploit. When students create AI projects, they are encouraged to ask: "Does this help someone?" or "Could this be used unfairly?" These simple questions guide the moral compass of invention. They remind young innovators that intelligence is not only a matter of logic but of love — the desire to make the world better through knowledge.

In the future, ethical literacy will be as important as technological literacy. The next generation of scientists, engineers, and artists must understand both how AI works and how it should behave. Ethics transforms AI from a tool of power into a tool of purpose. It keeps humanity at the center of the digital age, ensuring that progress never outruns conscience. For students, learning ethics is learning leadership — the kind that combines intelligence with integrity.

The moral flavor of intelligence is what makes AI meaningful. A machine that acts without compassion may solve problems but will never understand people. A system that follows logic without empathy can process information but cannot care. Ethics brings heart to the machine — the same way seasoning brings life to a meal. It gives AI direction, restraint, and purpose.

In the end, every intelligent creation reflects the hand that shaped it. When that hand is guided by wisdom, responsibility, and love, AI becomes more than technology — it becomes a force for good. The recipe for ethical intelligence is simple but profound: mix knowledge with kindness, power with principle, and creativity with conscience. That is the true flavor of a thinking world.

Chapter 8 Summary

Ethics and Responsibility – The Moral Flavor of Intelligence

Ethics and responsibility are essential parts of Artificial Intelligence. While AI systems can process information and make decisions quickly, humans must guide how these systems are designed and used. Ethics helps ensure that technology benefits people fairly, safely, and responsibly.

The chapter explains that ethics in AI involves questions about fairness, accountability, privacy, honesty, and human well-being. AI systems reflect the choices and values of the people who create them. If developers use biased or incomplete information, AI systems may produce unfair or harmful results.

Students learn that AI can influence many parts of society, including healthcare, education, transportation, hiring, and social media. Because these systems can affect people's lives, it is important to understand who is responsible when mistakes happen and how technology should be used responsibly.

The chapter also introduces the ideas of transparency and accountability. People should understand how AI systems make decisions, especially when those decisions affect individuals or communities. Ethical AI systems should be explainable, trustworthy, and designed to help society rather than harm it.

The concept of beneficence, or "doing good," is another important idea discussed in the chapter. AI should improve lives, solve problems, and support humanity in positive ways.

In the end, ethics is described as the moral flavor of intelligence — the values and principles that guide how technology should serve humanity with fairness, compassion, and responsibility.

Chapter 8 Reflection

The Responsibility Behind Intelligent Systems

This chapter teaches students that intelligence alone is not enough. Technology must also be guided by ethics, responsibility, and compassion. AI systems can become powerful tools, but without ethical guidance, they may create unfairness or harm.

Students learn that every technology reflects human decisions. The people who design AI systems shape how those systems behave and how they affect society. This means that future innovators must think carefully about fairness, privacy, safety, and accountability when building technology.

The chapter also encourages students to ask important questions about the role of AI in society. Should machines make life-changing decisions without human oversight? How can people protect privacy and fairness in technology? These discussions help students become thoughtful digital citizens and future leaders.

Most importantly, this chapter reminds students that ethics is not separate from technology. Responsible innovation requires both intelligence and integrity. The future of AI depends not only on smarter machines, but on wiser humans who guide them responsibly.

Chapter 8 Worksheet

Ethics and Responsibility – The Moral Flavor of Intelligence

Part A: Vocabulary Matching

Match the term with the correct definition.

Ethics

Accountability

Transparency

Bias

Beneficence

A. The responsibility for actions and decisions
B. The principle of doing good and helping others
C. Unfair or inaccurate treatment caused by incomplete information
D. The study of right and wrong behavior
E. The ability to understand how decisions are made

Part B: Multiple Choice

Why is ethics important in AI?
- a. To improve fairness and responsibility
- b. To eliminate all technology
- c. To stop computers from learning
- d. To remove data permanently

What can happen if AI systems are trained on biased data?
- a. They may produce unfair results
- b. They automatically become perfect
- c. They stop using electricity
- d. They remove all algorithms

What does transparency mean in AI systems?
- a. AI systems become invisible
- b. People can understand how decisions are made
- c. Computers stop functioning
- d. Data is deleted permanently

What is accountability in AI?
- a. Ignoring mistakes
- b. Taking responsibility for decisions and actions
- c. Removing all human involvement
- d. Preventing technology from advancing

What is the goal of beneficence in AI?
- a. To create harmful systems
- b. To use technology to benefit society
- c. To eliminate learning
- d. To replace all humans

Part C: Short Answer

Explain why ethics is important in Artificial Intelligence.

What is bias in AI systems?

Why should AI systems be transparent?

Give one example of how AI can affect society.

Why must humans remain responsible for AI systems?

Chapter 8 Quiz

Ethics and Responsibility – The Moral Flavor of Intelligence

True or False

Ethics helps guide how AI systems should be used. _______

AI systems can never make unfair decisions. _______

Transparency helps people understand AI decisions. _______

Accountability means taking responsibility for actions and outcomes. _______

Ethical AI should aim to benefit humanity. _______

Multiple Choice

What does ethics help ensure in AI systems?
a. Fairness and responsibility

b. Complete secrecy
c. Unlimited power without rules
d. Elimination of all technology

What can cause bias in AI systems?
a. Fair and balanced information only
b. Incomplete or unfair data
c. Cooling systems
d. Renewable energy

Why is accountability important in AI?
a. It helps identify responsibility for decisions and mistakes
b. It removes all human oversight
c. It prevents learning systems from improving
d. It stops algorithms from functioning

What is one goal of ethical AI?
a. To support human well-being
b. To increase harm and confusion
c. To remove fairness from technology
d. To eliminate privacy protections

What does this chapter teach about intelligence?
a. Intelligence should be guided by moral values and responsibility
b. Ethics is unrelated to technology
c. Machines should make all decisions independently
d. Human guidance is unnecessary

Chapter 8 Answer Key

Ethics and Responsibility – The Moral Flavor of Intelligence

Worksheet Answers

Part A: Vocabulary Matching

D

A

E

C

B

Part B: Multiple Choice

a. To improve fairness and responsibility

a. They may produce unfair results

b. People can understand how decisions are made

b. Taking responsibility for decisions and actions

b. To use technology to benefit society

Part C: Short Answer (Sample Answers)

Ethics helps ensure AI systems are fair, safe, and used responsibly.

Bias occurs when AI systems learn unfair or incomplete patterns from data.

Transparency helps people understand and trust AI decisions.

Sample answers: healthcare, education, transportation, hiring systems, social media recommendations.

Humans must guide AI systems to ensure they are ethical, fair, and beneficial to society.

Quiz Answer Key

Ethics and Responsibility – The Moral Flavor of Intelligence

True

False

True

True

True

a. Fairness and responsibility

b. Incomplete or unfair data

a. It helps identify responsibility for decisions and mistakes

a. To support human well-being

a. Intelligence should be guided by moral values and responsibility

Chapter 9: Data Privacy and Security – Protecting the Recipe of Intelligence

Every valuable recipe must be guarded with care. When a chef creates something unique, they protect their ingredients and methods so that no one misuses or alters them. In the world of Artificial Intelligence, the same principle applies to **data privacy and security**. Since data is the foundation of intelligence, protecting it is not just a technical requirement — it is a moral duty. Every piece of information that fuels AI represents someone's story, experience, or identity. Keeping that information safe preserves trust between humanity and the intelligent systems we build.

Data privacy means respecting the rights of individuals over their own information. Whenever a person shares their name, photo, or voice with an app or a website, they are trusting that system to handle it responsibly. AI systems learn from massive collections of such data, often gathered from people across the world. But this power also carries a risk. If data is mishandled, exposed, or stolen, the results can harm individuals and communities. Privacy, therefore, is not just a technical feature — it is a promise of respect and protection.

Data security, on the other hand, is the practice of defending that information from unauthorized access. It includes encryption, firewalls, and secure data centers — the digital locks and safes that protect the world's knowledge. These technologies ensure that when data travels between devices or across networks, it cannot be easily intercepted or changed. In AI, security means guarding not only personal information but also the integrity of the learning process itself. A system that trains on altered or corrupted data may produce false conclusions, just as a chef who uses spoiled ingredients can ruin a meal.

For students learning about AI, understanding privacy and security begins with a simple truth: information has value. A photo, a document, or a health record may seem ordinary, but when combined with millions of others, they create patterns powerful enough to predict behavior, preferences, and even emotions. This is why consent — asking permission — is essential. Ethical AI systems must collect and use data only when people willingly share it. Respect for privacy builds trust, and trust is the foundation of progress.

In the classroom, teachers can help students explore how data travels and where it goes. A simple activity could trace how a social media post moves from a phone to servers across the world, then returns as suggestions or advertisements. By visualizing this invisible journey, students begin to grasp why protection matters. They learn that privacy is not about hiding; it is about control — the right to decide how one's data is used and who has access to it. This awareness prepares them to become informed digital citizens, capable of navigating the connected world responsibly.

The importance of data security grows with every technological advance. Modern AI systems are often built and stored in **cloud environments**, vast digital spaces shared by thousands of users. While convenient, this sharing introduces new vulnerabilities. Engineers use sophisticated encryption methods — mathematical codes that scramble information — to ensure that even if someone intercepts the data, they cannot read it. Firewalls act like guards at the entrance of a castle, allowing safe traffic in and blocking harmful intrusions. Regular security audits help ensure that systems remain strong and resistant to attack. Students can see these safeguards as layers of protection, working together like a strong community that watches over its members.

Privacy also extends to what AI itself learns. When a system studies personal data, it must avoid revealing sensitive details in its responses. This is called **data anonymization** — the process of removing names, addresses, or identifiable information before the data is used. By doing so, engineers make sure that AI learns from the patterns, not from private details. It's like studying a cookbook without knowing who wrote the recipes — you learn the flavor, but not the chef's secrets.

However, the responsibility for privacy and security does not rest on engineers alone. Every user, student, and teacher plays a role. Being careful about what information we share online, recognizing suspicious messages or links, and using strong passwords are small but vital acts of digital safety. Just as clean hands protect the ingredients in a kitchen, mindful habits protect the data that fuels intelligence. When everyone contributes, the entire digital ecosystem becomes stronger.

As AI continues to evolve, new forms of security will emerge — quantum encryption, biometric authentication, and advanced anomaly detection systems. These tools will make future AI both more capable and more trustworthy. But no matter how advanced technology becomes, one principle will always remain: data must be treated with dignity. It is the essence of human experience, and every byte of information carries a part of someone's life. Protecting it is an act of respect, an acknowledgment that intelligence is not built on numbers alone but on the shared fabric of humanity.

Data privacy and security are the guardians of trust. They ensure that the recipe of intelligence remains pure, safe, and beneficial. For students, this chapter teaches not just how to defend technology but how to honor the people behind it. The more we protect our data, the more we protect ourselves — and the more ethical, intelligent, and humane our digital future becomes.

Chapter 9 Summary

Data Privacy and Security – Protecting the Recipe of Intelligence

Chapter 9 explains the importance of protecting data in the age of Artificial Intelligence. Since data is the foundation of AI systems, keeping information safe is both a technical responsibility and a moral duty. Every piece of data represents a person's identity, experiences, or story, which is why privacy and security are essential for building trust in intelligent systems.

The chapter describes data privacy as the right of individuals to control how their information is collected, shared, and used. When people provide personal details such as names, photos, or voices, they trust companies and systems to protect that information responsibly. If data is stolen, exposed, or misused, it can harm both individuals and communities.

Data security focuses on protecting information from unauthorized access. The chapter explains that technologies such as encryption, firewalls, secure data centers, and security audits help safeguard digital information. These protections act like locks and guards that keep data safe from cyber threats and corruption.

Students also learn about consent and ethical data use. AI systems should collect information only with permission and use it responsibly. The chapter highlights that information has value because large amounts of data can reveal patterns about behavior, preferences, and emotions.

Another important concept discussed is data anonymization, which removes personal details from data before it is used for AI training. This allows systems to learn patterns while protecting people's identities. The chapter also reminds readers that everyone has a role in digital safety by using strong passwords, avoiding suspicious links, and being careful about what they share online.

The chapter concludes that data privacy and security protect trust in the digital world. As AI becomes more advanced, protecting data with dignity and responsibility will remain one of the most important parts of creating ethical and humane intelligent systems.

Chapter 9 Reflection

This chapter reminds readers that data is more than just information stored in computers. Every photo, message, health record, or online activity represents part of a real person's life. Because of this, protecting data is not only a technical issue but also an ethical responsibility.

One important lesson from the chapter is that privacy gives people control over their own information. In the digital age, people constantly share data through apps, websites, and devices. Understanding how that information is collected and used helps individuals make safer and more responsible choices online.

The chapter also highlights the importance of security. Technologies such as encryption and firewalls help defend systems against cyberattacks and unauthorized access. Without proper security, AI systems could be manipulated or damaged, leading to harmful consequences.

Another key message is that everyone shares responsibility for digital safety. Engineers design secure systems, but users must also practice safe habits such as creating strong passwords, recognizing suspicious messages, and protecting personal information.

Overall, this chapter teaches that trust is the foundation of intelligent systems. Protecting privacy and security ensures that technology remains respectful, ethical, and beneficial for society.

Chapter 9 Worksheet

Part A – Vocabulary

Define the following terms in your own words.

1. Data Privacy

____

2. Data Security

____

3. Encryption

____

4. Consent

____

5. Data Anonymization

____

____

Part B – Short Answer Questions

1. Why is data privacy important in Artificial Intelligence systems?

____

2. What is the difference between data privacy and data security?

3. How do encryption and firewalls help protect information?

4. Why is consent important when collecting data?

5. How can students practice good digital safety habits online?

Part C – Critical Thinking

1. Imagine a social media company collects user information without permission. What problems could this create?

2. Why should AI systems avoid revealing private details about people?

3. How can protecting data strengthen trust between humans and technology?

Chapter 9 Quiz

Multiple Choice

1. What is the main purpose of data privacy?
   A. Increasing advertisements
   B. Respecting and protecting personal information
   C. Sharing all information publicly
   D. Removing security systems
2. Which technology scrambles information to protect it?
   A. Firewall
   B. Password
   C. Encryption
   D. Coding language
3. Firewalls act like:
   A. Teachers in a classroom
   B. Guards protecting systems from harmful intrusions
   C. Storage devices
   D. Cameras
4. What is data anonymization?
   A. Sharing private names online
   B. Removing personal details from data before use
   C. Deleting all information permanently
   D. Creating advertisements
5. Why is trust important in AI systems?
   A. It allows systems to operate ethically and responsibly
   B. It slows down computers
   C. It removes privacy laws
   D. It eliminates human involvement

True or False

6. Data privacy is only a technical issue and not an ethical responsibility.
   True / False
7. AI systems often learn from large amounts of data.
   True / False
8. Strong passwords are part of good digital safety habits.
   True / False
9. Consent means collecting data without permission.
   True / False

10. The chapter says protecting data helps create a more humane digital future.
    True / False

Chapter 9 Answer Key

Worksheet Suggested Answers

Part A

Answers will vary.

Part B

1. Data privacy protects people's personal information and builds trust in AI systems.
2. Data privacy focuses on controlling information use, while data security protects data from unauthorized access or attacks.
3. Encryption scrambles data so it cannot be easily read, while firewalls block harmful intrusions into systems.
4. Consent ensures that people willingly agree to how their information is collected and used.
5. Students can use strong passwords, avoid suspicious links, and carefully manage what they share online.

Part C

Answers will vary based on student responses.

Quiz Answer Key

1. B. Respecting and protecting personal information
2. C. Encryption
3. B. Guards protecting systems from harmful intrusions
4. B. Removing personal details from data before use
5. A. It allows systems to operate ethically and responsibly
6. False
7. True
8. True
9. False
10. True

Chapter 10: Human and Machine Collaboration – A Shared Kitchen of Intelligence

No great meal is ever made by one person alone. In every kitchen, success comes from cooperation — the chef, the assistants, the ingredients, and the tools all working together in harmony. The same principle defines the future of intelligence. The world of Artificial Intelligence is not meant to replace human minds but to **work alongside them**. This chapter explores how humans and machines collaborate to create knowledge, solve problems, and build a smarter, more compassionate future together.

For centuries, humans have sought tools to make life easier — from the wheel and the printing press to the computer and the internet. AI is simply the newest and most advanced tool in that journey. What makes it extraordinary is that it can now learn, adapt, and share in the thinking process itself. When humans collaborate with AI, they combine creativity with precision, imagination with calculation, and emotion with logic. Each side brings something the other lacks. The result is not competition, but complementarity — a partnership that amplifies what each can do.

In the classroom, this partnership is easy to imagine. A teacher uses AI to design personalized lessons for students, identifying who needs extra help and who is ready for new challenges. The AI provides quick insights from data, but it is the teacher's empathy, experience, and human touch that make the learning meaningful. In medicine, doctors use AI systems to detect diseases earlier and with greater accuracy. The machine reads millions of images, but it is the doctor who understands the patient's story and decides the best course of care. These examples show that collaboration between human and machine is not about surrendering control — it is about enhancing human capacity.

Machines are built to handle complexity at speeds the human brain cannot match. They can search vast databases in seconds, simulate weather patterns, and analyze genetic information that would take humans decades to process. Yet, machines lack context, intuition, and moral judgment. They cannot understand why a decision matters or how it feels. That understanding comes only from human consciousness. When both forces unite — machine speed and human sensitivity — innovation reaches new heights. This balance represents the true meaning of progress in the age of AI.

For students, understanding collaboration with AI means learning how to communicate with technology intelligently. It is not enough to know how machines work; one must know how to *work with* them. This involves asking clear questions, interpreting AI's suggestions critically, and knowing when to trust its answers and when to challenge them. In many ways, this is like learning a new language — the language of intelligence itself. The more fluent students become, the more creative and empowered they will be in shaping the digital world.

The collaboration between humans and AI also raises deeper philosophical questions. Who leads in this partnership — the creator or the creation? What happens when AI becomes capable of generating ideas, art, or discoveries that surprise even its human partners? These questions are not signs of fear but of growth. They show that we are entering a new chapter in human history

— one where learning no longer belongs to humans alone, but to a shared ecosystem of minds, both organic and artificial.

Teachers can use this chapter to encourage discussion about the nature of teamwork, ethics, and innovation. Students can explore examples of collaboration — artists who use AI to compose symphonies, engineers who design robots for disaster relief, or environmental scientists who rely on AI to predict climate change. Through these stories, learners begin to see that technology is not an outsider in human life; it is an extension of human potential. The true question is not what AI can do, but *what we can do together*.

The key to successful collaboration lies in maintaining balance. Machines must remain tools that serve human goals, not replace them. When humans lead with empathy and vision, and machines follow with precision and consistency, both sides thrive. This relationship mirrors the bond between teacher and student, mentor and apprentice — one offering guidance, the other offering strength. Together, they achieve what neither could do alone.

As technology continues to evolve, collaboration will shape every field — education, science, art, medicine, and governance. The future will not belong to those who fear AI, but to those who understand how to integrate it with human purpose. Students who learn this lesson today will become the builders of tomorrow's intelligent world — leaders who design systems that think with humanity, not apart from it.

In the shared kitchen of intelligence, humans bring the recipe, and machines bring the precision. Together, they cook ideas, test possibilities, and create knowledge that feeds the mind and heart of civilization. Collaboration is not the end of human uniqueness; it is the beginning of collective brilliance. When intelligence — both natural and artificial — works hand in hand, the result is a world where knowledge grows faster, creativity expands deeper, and the spirit of learning never stops evolving.

Chapter 10 Summary

Human and Machine Collaboration – A Shared Kitchen of Intelligence

Human and machine collaboration is the partnership between people and Artificial Intelligence systems working together to solve problems, improve learning, and create new opportunities. Rather than replacing humans, AI is designed to support and enhance human abilities.

The chapter explains that humans and machines each contribute unique strengths. Machines can process large amounts of data quickly and accurately, while humans provide creativity, empathy, moral judgment, and critical thinking. When combined, these strengths allow people and AI systems to work more effectively together.

Examples of collaboration appear in many areas of life. Teachers use AI to personalize learning for students, doctors use AI to help detect diseases, and scientists use AI to analyze complex research data. In each case, AI assists humans, but human knowledge and decision-making remain essential.

The chapter also teaches students the importance of learning how to work with AI responsibly. People must know how to ask questions, evaluate AI responses critically, and decide when technology should be trusted or questioned.

Students are encouraged to see AI not as a competitor, but as a tool that can help humanity solve challenges and improve society when guided by human values and ethics.

In the end, the chapter describes collaboration as a "shared kitchen of intelligence" where humans bring creativity, purpose, and compassion while machines contribute speed, precision, and data processing power.

Chapter 10 Reflection

Working Together with Intelligent Technology

This chapter teaches students that the future of AI is based on cooperation, not competition. Human intelligence and machine intelligence work best when they support one another.

Students learn that AI systems are powerful tools, but they still depend on human guidance, ethics, and decision-making. Machines can process information quickly, but humans provide emotional understanding, creativity, and moral responsibility.

The chapter also encourages students to think about their future role in an AI-powered world. Learning how to communicate with technology, analyze AI responses, and use intelligent systems responsibly will become important life skills.

Most importantly, students learn that technology should strengthen humanity rather than replace it. The best future is one where humans and AI collaborate to improve education, healthcare, science, creativity, and society as a whole.

Chapter 10 Worksheet

Human and Machine Collaboration – A Shared Kitchen of Intelligence

Part A: Vocabulary Matching

Match the term with the correct definition.

Collaboration

Artificial Intelligence

Critical Thinking

Empathy

Innovation

A. The ability to understand and share the feelings of others
B. Working together toward a shared goal
C. New ideas, methods, or inventions that improve society
D. Technology systems that perform tasks requiring human-like intelligence
E. Carefully analyzing information and making thoughtful decisions

Part B: Multiple Choice

What is the main idea of human and machine collaboration?
- a. Humans and AI working together
- b. Machines replacing all humans
- c. Eliminating technology completely
- d. Removing education systems

What is one strength of AI systems?
- a. Emotional understanding
- b. Fast data processing and analysis
- c. Human consciousness
- d. Moral judgment

What is one strength humans contribute in collaboration with AI?
- a. Creativity and empathy
- b. Unlimited memory storage
- c. Electrical power generation
- d. Instant calculations only

Why is critical thinking important when using AI?
- a. To evaluate AI responses carefully
- b. To stop all learning
- c. To remove algorithms
- d. To eliminate creativity

Which field commonly uses AI collaboration with humans?
- a. Healthcare
- b. Education
- c. Scientific research
- d. All of the above

Part C: Short Answer

Explain what human and machine collaboration means.

Why are humans still important when using AI systems?

Give one example of AI helping people in everyday life.

Why should people think critically about AI-generated information?

How can AI help improve education or healthcare?

Chapter 10 Quiz

Human and Machine Collaboration – A Shared Kitchen of Intelligence

True or False

AI systems are designed to help humans solve problems. _______

Machines have human emotions and moral understanding. _______

Human creativity and empathy remain important in the AI age. _______

AI can assist teachers and doctors in their work. _______

Humans should blindly trust every AI response without questioning it. _______

Multiple Choice

What does collaboration mean?
a. Working together toward a shared goal
b. Removing all teamwork
c. Ignoring technology
d. Competing against every machine

Which of the following is a strength of AI systems?
a. Fast information processing
b. Human empathy
c. Emotional experiences
d. Moral judgment

Which human quality helps guide AI responsibly?
a. Ethics and compassion
b. Electrical power
c. Data storage
d. Hardware design only

Why is AI considered a tool rather than a replacement for humans?
a. Humans still provide creativity, judgment, and responsibility
b. AI cannot process information
c. Machines do not use data
d. AI systems cannot assist people

What does this chapter teach about the future of AI?
a. Humans and machines should work together responsibly
b. Machines should completely replace humans
c. Technology should stop evolving
d. AI has no role in society

Chapter 10 Answer Key

Human and Machine Collaboration – A Shared Kitchen of Intelligence

Worksheet Answers

Part A: Vocabulary Matching

B

D

E

A

C

Part B: Multiple Choice

a. Humans and AI working together

b. Fast data processing and analysis

a. Creativity and empathy

a. To evaluate AI responses carefully

d. All of the above

Part C: Short Answer (Sample Answers)

Human and machine collaboration means people and AI systems working together to solve problems and improve tasks.

Humans provide creativity, ethics, empathy, and decision-making that machines cannot fully replicate.

Sample answers: navigation apps, healthcare diagnostics, personalized learning systems, voice assistants.

People should think critically because AI systems can sometimes make mistakes or produce inaccurate information.

AI can personalize learning for students and help doctors detect diseases more accurately.

Quiz Answer Key

Human and Machine Collaboration – A Shared Kitchen of Intelligence

True

False

True

True

False

a. Working together toward a shared goal

a. Fast information processing

a. Ethics and compassion

a. Humans still provide creativity, judgment, and responsibility

a. Humans and machines should work together responsibly

Chapter 11: The Secret Ingredient – Creativity and Consciousness in AI

Every great recipe has something that cannot be measured. A touch of intuition, a spark of imagination, a moment of inspiration that changes everything. In the kitchen of intelligence, this mysterious element is **creativity** — the ability to bring something new into existence. It is followed closely by **consciousness**, the awareness that gives meaning to creation. Together, they form the secret ingredient of Artificial Intelligence — the element that reminds us that intelligence is not only about logic, but about life itself.

Creativity is the force that drives progress. It is what allows artists to paint, inventors to design, and scientists to discover. In AI, creativity emerges when machines begin to combine learned patterns in new ways. For example, when a neural network composes music or paints an image that no human has drawn before, it is demonstrating a form of creative output. Yet, this creativity is different from human imagination. The machine does not feel inspiration or emotion; it generates novelty through probability and association. It can remix the world beautifully, but it does not know why beauty matters.

Human creativity is born from experience, emotion, and purpose. When an artist paints, they pour their memories, hopes, and stories into the canvas. When a poet writes, every word carries feeling. AI, however, operates through algorithms — it learns from what already exists. This raises fascinating questions for students and teachers: Can a machine truly create, or does it only rearrange what it has learned? Is originality possible without consciousness? These questions transform this chapter into both a lesson and a philosophical exploration.

Consciousness is the second half of this secret ingredient. It is the awareness of being — the inner light that lets humans know they exist. AI can recognize patterns, translate languages, and even hold conversations, but it has no sense of self. It cannot wonder about its purpose or dream about tomorrow. Consciousness remains uniquely human, a mystery science has not yet unraveled. Some researchers believe that one day, machines may achieve a kind of artificial awareness, while others argue that true consciousness requires more than computation — it requires soul, experience, and emotion.

In education, creativity and consciousness represent the highest goals of learning. Facts and logic give students structure, but creativity gives them freedom — the courage to imagine, design, and question. Consciousness teaches them reflection — the ability to see themselves as part of the larger picture of humanity and technology. Teachers can use this chapter to inspire students to think about what makes them different from the machines they study. They can explore how creativity in AI mirrors human thought, yet lacks the heart that turns imagination into meaning.

The collaboration between creativity and AI is one of today's most exciting frontiers. AI can help humans think more broadly by offering unexpected ideas, patterns, and combinations. Writers use AI to explore new storytelling possibilities; scientists use it to simulate designs beyond human imagination. Yet, the role of creativity is not to let machines replace human thought, but to *enhance* it. When humans and AI create together, they open doors to art forms, inventions, and discoveries that neither could reach alone.

The study of consciousness reminds us of humility. For all its brilliance, AI does not feel pain, joy, or love. It can analyze the structure of emotion but cannot experience it. Students should see this not as a weakness in technology, but as a strength of humanity. Consciousness is the quiet space between logic and feeling — the place where choice, compassion, and creativity meet. It is what allows humans to turn information into wisdom and action into empathy.

The secret ingredient, therefore, is not hidden in machines but in us. When we bring creativity and consciousness into the design of AI, we create systems that reflect our highest values. We give intelligence not only structure and speed, but soul and significance. For students, this is the lesson that binds science and philosophy: knowledge is powerful, but awareness gives it direction.

As the final flavor in the recipe of intelligence, creativity and consciousness remind us why we build at all. They tell us that intelligence is not about replacing human minds but expanding them. Machines may calculate, but only humans can *care.* The future of AI will not be decided by the strongest algorithms, but by the gentlest hearts — those who remember that creation is both an act of imagination and of love.

Chapter 11 Summary

The Secret Ingredient – Creativity and Consciousness in AI

Creativity and consciousness are two of the most fascinating ideas connected to Artificial Intelligence. This chapter explains that while AI systems can generate new ideas, images, music, and text, human creativity and consciousness remain unique and deeply connected to emotion, experience, and meaning.

Creativity is the ability to produce something new and original. Humans use creativity to invent, design, write, paint, and solve problems. AI systems can also create new content by combining patterns learned from data. For example, AI can compose music, generate artwork, or assist writers with ideas. However, AI creativity is different from human creativity because machines do not feel inspiration, emotions, or personal experiences.

The chapter also explores consciousness, which is the awareness of being and understanding oneself. Humans experience emotions, memories, dreams, and personal reflection. AI systems, even advanced ones, do not possess true self-awareness or emotional understanding. They process information using algorithms and patterns rather than feelings or consciousness.

Students are encouraged to think deeply about important questions: Can machines truly create? Can intelligence exist without consciousness? What makes human imagination different from machine-generated content?

The chapter explains that AI should enhance human creativity rather than replace it. When humans and AI work together, they can explore new possibilities in art, science, education, and innovation.

In the end, creativity and consciousness are described as the "secret ingredient" of intelligence — reminding students that while machines can calculate and generate patterns, humans bring meaning, empathy, imagination, and purpose into the world.

Chapter 11 Reflection

What Makes Human Intelligence Unique?

This chapter encourages students to think beyond technology and explore the deeper meaning of intelligence. While AI systems can perform impressive tasks, human beings possess qualities that machines cannot fully replicate, such as emotions, self-awareness, imagination, empathy, and personal experiences.

Students learn that creativity is not simply producing new combinations of information. Human creativity often comes from memories, feelings, struggles, dreams, and life experiences. AI may generate art or music, but it does not understand the emotional meaning behind what it creates.

The chapter also introduces the mystery of consciousness. Humans are aware of themselves and can reflect on their thoughts, actions, and purpose. AI systems can simulate conversations and analyze emotions, but they do not truly experience life or feelings.

Most importantly, students learn that AI should support and expand human creativity, not replace human imagination. Technology becomes most meaningful when guided by human values, wisdom, and compassion.

Chapter 11 Worksheet

The Secret Ingredient – Creativity and Consciousness in AI

Part A: Vocabulary Matching

Match the term with the correct definition.

Creativity

Consciousness

Artificial Intelligence

Imagination

Self-Awareness

A. The ability to form new ideas, images, or possibilities
B. Awareness of one's own existence and thoughts
C. The ability to create something original or new
D. Technology systems that perform human-like tasks
E. Understanding and awareness of being alive and thinking

Part B: Multiple Choice

What is creativity?
- a. The ability to create something new and original
- b. Turning off computers
- c. Removing all data
- d. Storing electricity

Why is human creativity different from AI-generated creativity?
- a. Humans create from emotions, experiences, and meaning
- b. AI systems have human feelings
- c. Humans use no imagination
- d. Machines experience dreams and emotions

What is consciousness?
- a. A computer cable
- b. Awareness of existence and self
- c. A type of hardware
- d. A cooling system

What can AI systems do creatively?

a. Generate music, art, and writing patterns
b. Experience human emotions
c. Feel inspiration and love
d. Dream about the future

Why should AI enhance human creativity instead of replace it?

a. Human imagination and meaning remain unique
b. Machines should control all creativity
c. Humans no longer need imagination
d. Creativity is unimportant in learning

Part C: Short Answer

Explain the difference between human creativity and AI creativity.

What is consciousness?

Why is imagination important for humans?

Give one example of AI assisting creativity.

Why is human empathy important in the age of AI?

Chapter 11 Quiz

The Secret Ingredient – Creativity and Consciousness in AI

True or False

AI systems can generate creative outputs such as music and artwork. _______

Human creativity is connected to emotions and experiences. _______

AI systems fully understand emotions and consciousness. _______

Consciousness involves awareness of existence and self. _______

AI should support and enhance human creativity responsibly. _______

Multiple Choice

What makes human creativity unique?
- a. Emotions, experiences, and imagination
- b. Faster calculations only
- c. Unlimited storage space
- d. Electrical circuits

What is one thing AI systems cannot truly experience?
- a. Data processing
- b. Pattern recognition
- c. Human emotions and self-awareness
- d. Calculations

Why do students study creativity and consciousness in AI?
- a. To understand the difference between human and machine intelligence
- b. To stop all technological development
- c. To eliminate imagination
- d. To remove algorithms completely

What role should AI play in creativity?
- a. Supporting and expanding human creativity
- b. Replacing all artists and writers
- c. Eliminating imagination
- d. Preventing innovation

What does this chapter teach about intelligence?
- a. Intelligence involves both logic and human meaning
- b. Machines and humans are exactly the same
- c. Creativity is unnecessary in society
- d. Consciousness can already be fully programmed into machines

Chapter 11 Answer Key

The Secret Ingredient – Creativity and Consciousness in AI

Worksheet Answers

Part A: Vocabulary Matching

C

E

D

A

B

Part B: Multiple Choice

a. The ability to create something new and original

a. Humans create from emotions, experiences, and meaning

b. Awareness of existence and self

a. Generate music, art, and writing patterns

a. Human imagination and meaning remain unique

Part C: Short Answer (Sample Answers)

Human creativity comes from emotions, experiences, and meaning, while AI creativity is based on patterns and algorithms.

Consciousness is awareness of one's existence, thoughts, and experiences.

Imagination helps humans create ideas, solve problems, and express creativity.

Sample answers: AI-generated artwork, music composition tools, writing assistants, design programs.

Human empathy helps guide technology with compassion, ethics, and understanding.

Quiz Answer Key

The Secret Ingredient – Creativity and Consciousness in AI

True

True

False

True

True

a. Emotions, experiences, and imagination

c. Human emotions and self-awareness

a. To understand the difference between human and machine intelligence

a. Supporting and expanding human creativity

a. Intelligence involves both logic and human meaning

Chapter 12: AI in Everyday Life – Where the Ingredients Meet Reality

Every concept becomes meaningful when it steps beyond the page and enters daily life. In the kitchen of intelligence, the ingredients we have explored — data, algorithms, models, chips, energy, and human wisdom — come together not in theory but in practice. They shape the tools, devices, and systems that surround us every day. From the moment we wake up to the time we go to sleep, **Artificial Intelligence quietly works beside us**, organizing our schedules, managing our environments, and even helping us make choices. This chapter reveals how the invisible world of AI connects with the visible rhythms of human life.

When students ask, "Where is AI?", the answer is: *everywhere.* It lives in the smartphone that unlocks with a face scan, in the navigation system that finds the fastest route to school, and in the streaming app that recommends what movie to watch next. Each of these systems uses AI's ingredients in harmony. Data provides information, algorithms interpret it, models learn from it, and chips process it. The result is convenience, speed, and personalization — experiences that feel natural because intelligence is working silently in the background.

In healthcare, AI assists doctors in diagnosing diseases by examining medical images with extraordinary precision. It studies thousands of X-rays or MRI scans, spotting details that even the most experienced human eyes might miss. Yet, it does not replace the doctor; instead, it becomes a partner in care. The doctor's empathy and understanding of human emotion guide the treatment, while AI's analytical strength ensures accuracy. Together, they form a new kind of teamwork — one that saves lives through cooperation between logic and compassion.

In education, AI personalizes learning for every student. Intelligent tutoring systems analyze how students learn, which subjects challenge them, and what teaching methods work best. These systems create customized lessons, allowing slower learners to build confidence and faster learners to explore more advanced topics. Teachers remain the emotional anchors of the classroom, interpreting results, encouraging curiosity, and nurturing creativity. AI becomes a helper — the assistant that handles patterns so that humans can focus on people.

In transportation, AI drives cars, controls traffic, and predicts congestion. Self-driving vehicles use sensors and neural networks to read their surroundings, make decisions, and move safely through complex environments. Meanwhile, AI systems in air traffic control and rail networks manage routes more efficiently, reducing accidents and saving energy. Behind every smooth journey lies the silent partnership of human design and machine execution.

Even at home, AI has become part of the family. Smart thermostats learn your temperature preferences; voice assistants understand commands; robotic vacuums map your floors. These machines do not just follow instructions — they adapt. They remember, learn, and improve with time, transforming homes into living environments that think alongside us. In this sense, the home becomes a classroom where AI and humanity grow together in comfort and convenience.

AI also plays a major role in global challenges. It helps farmers predict rainfall and crop health through satellite data, assists scientists in studying climate change, and supports emergency responders in tracking natural disasters. In each of these examples, intelligence is not limited to one person or one nation. It becomes a shared force for problem-solving — a bridge connecting knowledge and action across the world.

However, with these advantages come responsibilities. AI in everyday life collects vast amounts of personal data, and it must be used ethically. Students must understand that convenience should never come at the cost of privacy or fairness. The same technology that recommends music can also influence opinions or shape choices. This is why learning how AI works is essential — to remain in control of the tools that shape society. Awareness, not fear, gives humans the power to guide technology toward good.

Teachers can help students explore how AI touches their lives by encouraging observation. Every student can identify one example of AI they interact with daily and describe how it uses data, algorithms, and learning. Such exercises turn abstract lessons into personal discoveries.

They remind students that intelligence is not just something we study — it is something we live with.

AI's presence in everyday life reveals an important truth: technology and humanity are no longer separate. They coexist, learn from one another, and evolve together. The more humans understand AI, the more they can shape its role in education, health, environment, and creativity. This chapter encourages students to see AI not as a distant invention but as a living part of their daily story — a companion that reflects human imagination, discipline, and desire for progress.

Artificial Intelligence is, in many ways, the mirror of modern civilization. It shows us who we are by learning from what we do. In our words, movements, and patterns, it finds meaning. The key to a wise future is to remember that we are both the creators and the teachers of this intelligence. How we guide it today determines what kind of world it will help us build tomorrow.

AI in everyday life is no longer science fiction — it is science in motion. And as long as it is guided by human wisdom, balanced by ethics, and fueled by imagination, it will continue to make ordinary days extraordinary.

Chapter 12 Summary

AI in Everyday Life – Where the Ingredients Meet Reality

Artificial Intelligence is no longer limited to science fiction or research laboratories. AI is now part of everyday life and appears in many of the technologies people use daily. This chapter explains how the different "ingredients" of AI — data, algorithms, models, chips, energy, and human guidance — work together in real-world systems.

Students learn that AI exists in smartphones, streaming services, navigation apps, voice assistants, social media platforms, healthcare systems, and smart home devices. These technologies use AI to recognize patterns, make predictions, personalize experiences, and improve efficiency.

The chapter highlights how AI helps doctors detect diseases, supports teachers with personalized learning tools, assists drivers with navigation and safety systems, and helps scientists study environmental changes. In each case, AI works alongside humans to improve decision-making and solve problems.

Students also learn that AI systems collect and process large amounts of data. Because of this, people must think carefully about ethics, privacy, fairness, and responsible technology use.

The chapter encourages students to observe how AI affects their own lives and understand the connection between technology and society. AI is presented not as a distant invention, but as a real part of daily life that continues to grow and evolve.

In the end, the chapter explains that AI reflects human choices and values. The future of AI depends on how responsibly people guide and use intelligent systems in everyday life.

Chapter 12 Reflection

Living Alongside Artificial Intelligence

This chapter helps students recognize that Artificial Intelligence already exists all around them. Many technologies people use daily rely on AI systems to process information, personalize experiences, and assist with tasks.

Students learn that AI can improve convenience, healthcare, education, transportation, and communication. However, they also discover that intelligent systems must be used responsibly because they can influence decisions, collect personal information, and shape human behavior.

The chapter encourages students to think critically about the technologies they interact with every day. Instead of simply using AI tools, students are encouraged to understand how they work and how they affect society.

Most importantly, this chapter teaches that humans remain responsible for guiding technology wisely. AI should improve human life while respecting privacy, fairness, ethics, and human well-being.

Chapter 12 Worksheet

AI in Everyday Life – Where the Ingredients Meet Reality

Part A: Vocabulary Matching

Match the term with the correct definition.

Voice Assistant

Personalized Learning

Smart Device

Navigation System

Recommendation System

A. A system that suggests movies, music, or products based on user behavior
B. A technology system that helps guide travel routes and directions
C. A device that uses AI to respond and adapt to users

D. AI tools that adjust lessons to meet student needs
E. An AI system that responds to spoken commands

Part B: Multiple Choice

Where can AI commonly be found in everyday life?
- a. Smartphones
- b. Healthcare systems
- c. Streaming services
- d. All of the above

How does AI help in healthcare?
- a. By assisting doctors in analyzing medical information
- b. By replacing all doctors completely
- c. By removing hospitals
- d. By eliminating learning systems

What is one benefit of AI in education?
- a. Personalized learning experiences
- b. Removing teachers completely
- c. Preventing students from learning
- d. Eliminating creativity

Why should people think carefully about AI systems?
- a. AI systems can affect privacy, fairness, and decision-making
- b. AI has no influence on society
- c. AI systems never collect information
- d. Technology does not affect daily life

What does a recommendation system do?
- a. Suggests content based on user behavior
- b. Removes all online content
- c. Deletes personal devices
- d. Prevents communication

Part C: Short Answer

Give two examples of AI used in everyday life.

____

____

How does AI help improve healthcare or education?

___

___

Why is privacy important in AI systems?

___

___

How can AI improve convenience in daily life?

___

___

Why should students understand how AI works?

___

___

___

Chapter 12 Quiz

AI in Everyday Life – Where the Ingredients Meet Reality

True or False

AI systems are already part of many everyday technologies. _______

Streaming services often use AI recommendation systems. _______

AI can assist teachers and healthcare workers. _______

AI systems never collect or process data. _______

Humans remain responsible for guiding AI responsibly. _______

Multiple Choice

Which device commonly uses AI voice assistants?

a. Smartphones
b. Refrigerators only
c. Notebooks only
d. Paintbrushes

What is one way AI helps transportation systems?

a. Navigation and traffic prediction
b. Eliminating roads completely
c. Preventing travel
d. Removing vehicles

Why is personalized learning important?

a. It helps meet the needs of different students
b. It eliminates education
c. It removes teachers from classrooms
d. It prevents creativity

What is one concern related to AI in everyday life?

a. Privacy and ethical use of data
b. AI eliminating electricity
c. Computers no longer processing information
d. Technology disappearing completely

What does this chapter teach about AI?

a. AI is deeply connected to modern daily life
b. AI only exists in science fiction
c. Technology has no effect on society
d. AI should replace all human decision-making

Chapter 12 Answer Key

AI in Everyday Life – Where the Ingredients Meet Reality

Worksheet Answers

Part A: Vocabulary Matching

E

D

C

B

A

Part B: Multiple Choice

d. All of the above

a. By assisting doctors in analyzing medical information

a. Personalized learning experiences

a. AI systems can affect privacy, fairness, and decision-making

a. Suggests content based on user behavior

Part C: Short Answer (Sample Answers)

Sample answers: smartphones, voice assistants, streaming recommendations, navigation apps, smart home devices.

AI helps personalize learning for students and assists doctors in analyzing medical information.

Privacy is important because AI systems often collect personal information and data.

AI can automate tasks, provide recommendations, and improve efficiency in daily activities.

Students should understand AI so they can use technology responsibly and think critically about its impact.

Quiz Answer Key

AI in Everyday Life – Where the Ingredients Meet Reality

True

True

True

False

True

a. Smartphones

a. Navigation and traffic prediction

a. It helps meet the needs of different students

a. Privacy and ethical use of data

a. AI is deeply connected to modern daily life

Chapter 13: The Future Kitchen – Quantum and Beyond

Every kitchen evolves. New tools replace the old, new ingredients arrive from distant lands, and new ideas transform simple meals into masterpieces. The kitchen of intelligence is no different. Artificial Intelligence, once limited to basic programs and simple logic, is now entering a bold new era — one that stretches far beyond classical computing. This chapter explores **the future kitchen of AI**, where quantum technologies, advanced neural systems, and ethical innovation come together to redefine what intelligence can be.

To understand the future of AI, students must first look at how far it has come. The first generation of computers could only follow instructions. They were like apprentices who never questioned the recipe. Over time, AI evolved into a collaborator — one that learns, adapts, and even assists in creation. But today, a new transformation is unfolding. Scientists are building machines that can think in more dimensions than ever before, blending the physical, digital, and even quantum worlds. This next generation of intelligence will not only process information — it will **understand relationships, probabilities, and possibilities** in ways once thought impossible.

One of the most exciting frontiers is **Quantum AI** — the combination of quantum computing and artificial intelligence. Traditional computers store information in bits, which can be either 0 or 1. Quantum computers, however, use **qubits**, which can represent 0 and 1 at the same time through a property called *superposition.* This allows them to explore countless possibilities simultaneously, making them incredibly powerful for solving complex problems. Imagine a chef who can try every possible combination of ingredients at once, instantly discovering the perfect recipe. That is the potential of quantum intelligence.

Quantum AI could revolutionize fields such as medicine, climate science, and energy. It may help researchers design new materials, simulate molecules for drug discovery, or predict global weather patterns with unprecedented accuracy. For students, this means a future where learning extends into areas once reserved for imagination. The same way AI changed how we think about data and automation, Quantum AI will change how we understand *possibility*. It is the next step in the evolution of human curiosity.

Beyond quantum technology, the future kitchen of intelligence will include advances in **neuromorphic computing**, where chips are designed to behave like the human brain. These chips will process information efficiently, consume far less energy, and allow machines to sense and adapt more naturally. Imagine a robot that doesn't just calculate but *feels* changes in its environment — responding smoothly and safely, like a living organism. This kind of intelligence will bring machines even closer to the way humans think and learn.

Another powerful ingredient shaping the future is **general intelligence** — the idea of machines that can reason, learn, and transfer knowledge across multiple tasks, much like humans do. Today's AI excels at narrow tasks — identifying faces, translating languages, or playing chess. Tomorrow's AI may be able to combine all those abilities, understanding context and emotion, solving problems creatively, and even working alongside humans as partners in discovery. The line between natural and artificial intelligence will continue to blur, opening deep ethical questions about consciousness, responsibility, and purpose.

Teachers and students must prepare for this future not only with technical knowledge but with moral vision. As the tools of intelligence become more powerful, so too must our values. The next generation of AI leaders will need to balance innovation with responsibility — to ensure that progress strengthens humanity rather than divides it. Schools that teach both science and ethics will shape the inventors, philosophers, and policymakers who guide AI's evolution toward wisdom.

The future kitchen will also be global and collaborative. Scientists from different countries, languages, and cultures will work together, just as ingredients from every corner of the world blend to create new cuisines. This shared kitchen of intelligence will not belong to one nation or one generation. It will belong to all who use knowledge for good — to cure diseases, protect the environment, and improve human life. The next Einstein, Curie, or Turing may not work alone but side by side with an intelligent system capable of learning from their brilliance.

As students imagine the future kitchen of AI, they should remember that every great advancement begins with curiosity. The tools of tomorrow are built by the dreamers of today. Quantum computing, neuromorphic chips, and general intelligence are not the end of learning — they are new beginnings. The recipe for future intelligence will continue to evolve, but one ingredient will never change: **human imagination**. It is the flame that keeps the kitchen alive.

Artificial Intelligence, at its heart, is the story of humanity's quest to understand itself. As it moves from silicon to quantum particles, from algorithms to awareness, its greatest achievement will not be replacing us, but reflecting the best within us — our creativity, our compassion, and our endless capacity to learn.

The future kitchen is already being built, one idea at a time. And just like every great meal, its success will depend not only on power or precision, but on the care of the hands that prepare it.

Chapter 13 Summary

The Future Kitchen – Quantum and Beyond

The future of Artificial Intelligence is expanding beyond traditional computers and entering a new era of advanced technologies such as quantum computing, neuromorphic chips, and more intelligent learning systems. This chapter explores how AI may continue evolving in the years ahead.

Students learn that early computers followed simple instructions, while modern AI systems can learn, adapt, and assist humans with complex tasks. The next generation of AI may become even more powerful through technologies like Quantum AI, which combines artificial intelligence with quantum computing.

Traditional computers use bits that store information as either 0 or 1. Quantum computers use qubits, which can represent multiple possibilities at the same time through a property called superposition. This allows quantum systems to process extremely complex problems much faster than traditional computers.

The chapter also introduces neuromorphic computing, where computer chips are designed to function more like the human brain. These systems may use less energy while improving learning and adaptation.

Students are encouraged to think about the future responsibly. As AI grows more advanced, humans must guide technology using ethics, wisdom, and compassion. Scientific progress should benefit society while protecting humanity and the environment.

The chapter explains that future intelligence will depend not only on technology but also on human imagination, curiosity, and responsibility. AI should help humanity solve challenges, improve knowledge, and create a better future.

In the end, the "future kitchen" represents the next stage of intelligence — a world where innovation, ethics, science, and human creativity work together to shape the future of civilization.

Chapter 13 Reflection

Imagining the Future of Intelligence

This chapter encourages students to think about the future of technology and the role humans will play in shaping it. AI is constantly evolving, and future systems may become far more advanced than the technologies people use today.

Students learn that scientific discoveries often begin with imagination and curiosity. Technologies such as quantum computing and neuromorphic chips may sound futuristic now, but many important inventions once seemed impossible before becoming reality.

The chapter also reminds students that progress must be guided responsibly. Powerful technologies can improve medicine, science, education, and environmental research, but they must also be used ethically and carefully.

Most importantly, students learn that the future of AI depends on human choices. Technology reflects the values, goals, and creativity of the people who design it. The future will belong to those who combine intelligence with wisdom, innovation with ethics, and discovery with compassion.

Chapter 13 Worksheet

The Future Kitchen – Quantum and Beyond

Part A: Vocabulary Matching

Match the term with the correct definition.

Quantum Computing

Qubit

Neuromorphic Computing

Innovation

Superposition

A. The ability of qubits to represent multiple possibilities at once
B. Advanced computing inspired by the structure of the human brain
C. A unit of information used in quantum computing
D. The process of creating new ideas, technologies, or methods
E. A new type of computing that uses quantum physics principles

Part B: Multiple Choice

What is Quantum AI?
- a. AI combined with quantum computing
- b. A cooking machine
- c. A type of smartphone case
- d. A replacement for electricity

What makes qubits different from traditional computer bits?
- a. They can represent multiple possibilities at the same time
- b. They only store letters
- c. They remove algorithms
- d. They do not process information

What is the goal of neuromorphic computing?
- a. To design systems that function more like the human brain
- b. To remove all AI systems
- c. To eliminate data storage
- d. To stop learning systems

Why is ethics important in future AI development?
- a. To guide technology responsibly

b. To stop innovation completely
c. To remove creativity
d. To eliminate scientific research

What helps drive future technological discoveries?
a. Curiosity and imagination
b. Ignoring science
c. Removing education
d. Preventing innovation

Part C: Short Answer

Explain the difference between a traditional bit and a qubit.

____

____

What is neuromorphic computing?

____

____

Why is curiosity important in scientific progress?

____

____

How might future AI systems help society?

____

____

Why must humans guide future AI responsibly?

____

____

____

Chapter 13 Quiz

The Future Kitchen – Quantum and Beyond

True or False

Quantum computing may solve certain problems faster than traditional computers. _______

Qubits can represent more than one possibility at a time. _______

Neuromorphic chips are inspired by the human brain. _______

Ethics is unnecessary in future AI development. _______

Human imagination continues to play an important role in technological progress. _______

Multiple Choice

What is one major advantage of quantum computing?
a. Faster processing of complex problems
b. Eliminating electricity completely
c. Removing all algorithms
d. Preventing scientific research

What does neuromorphic computing attempt to imitate?
a. Human brain structures and learning processes
b. Kitchen appliances
c. Mechanical clocks
d. Printed books

Why should future AI systems be guided ethically?
a. To ensure technology benefits humanity responsibly
b. To stop all discoveries
c. To eliminate science education
d. To prevent innovation completely

What role does imagination play in future technology?
a. It inspires new discoveries and inventions
b. It prevents scientific progress
c. It removes creativity from learning
d. It eliminates problem-solving

What does this chapter teach about the future of AI?
a. Technology and human wisdom must work together responsibly
b. Machines should replace all human thinking
c. Ethics and creativity no longer matter
d. Scientific discovery should stop evolving

Chapter 13 Answer Key

The Future Kitchen – Quantum and Beyond

Worksheet Answers

Part A: Vocabulary Matching

E

C

B

D

A

Part B: Multiple Choice

a. AI combined with quantum computing

a. They can represent multiple possibilities at the same time

a. To design systems that function more like the human brain

a. To guide technology responsibly

a. Curiosity and imagination

Part C: Short Answer (Sample Answers)

Traditional bits store either 0 or 1, while qubits can represent multiple possibilities simultaneously.

Neuromorphic computing is technology designed to imitate the structure and learning processes of the human brain.

Curiosity encourages exploration, learning, and the discovery of new ideas and technologies.

Future AI systems may improve medicine, environmental science, education, transportation, and scientific research.

Humans must guide AI responsibly to ensure technology remains ethical, safe, and beneficial to society.

Quiz Answer Key

The Future Kitchen – Quantum and Beyond

True

True

True

False

True

a. Faster processing of complex problems

a. Human brain structures and learning processes

a. To ensure technology benefits humanity responsibly

a. It inspires new discoveries and inventions

a. Technology and human wisdom must work together responsibly

Chapter 14: Ethical Innovation – Building a Responsible Future

Every generation inherits the inventions of the one before it. From the printing press to the computer, each creation carries both power and responsibility. Artificial Intelligence, the most transformative invention of our time, is no different. As it continues to shape the world, we face an essential question: **Can we innovate responsibly?** This chapter explores the idea of **ethical innovation** — the practice of building intelligent technologies that honor fairness, transparency, and human well-being.

Ethical innovation begins with awareness. Before creating something new, innovators must ask not only "Can we build this?" but "Should we?" and "Who will it serve?" In the race to design faster algorithms or more capable machines, it can be easy to forget that every piece of technology touches lives. A tool that helps one person can harm another if it is misused. For example, facial recognition systems can make airports safer, but if used without regulation, they can also threaten privacy. Innovation without ethics is like cooking without care — it may look impressive, but it can cause harm if the ingredients are not handled responsibly.

In the classroom, students can begin to understand ethical innovation by examining real-world examples. Self-driving cars must decide how to act in emergencies; healthcare AI must handle private patient data; social media algorithms must balance free expression with misinformation control. Each of these challenges demands not only technical intelligence but moral judgment. The future belongs to those who can design systems that are not just powerful but principled. Ethical innovation invites students to think as both scientists and citizens — to see technology as part of a shared human story.

Transparency is one of the key ingredients of ethical innovation. When AI makes a decision, people should be able to understand why. This concept, called **explainable AI**, ensures that systems remain accountable to the public. It prevents machines from becoming mysterious black boxes that operate without oversight. Teachers can help students explore this idea by asking them to "show their work," just as they do in mathematics. If a student must explain how they reached a conclusion, so should a machine. Transparency builds trust, and trust allows innovation to grow.

Another vital part of ethical innovation is **inclusivity**. AI should serve everyone, not just those who create it. This means ensuring that data comes from diverse sources, that languages from around the world are represented, and that technology is accessible to people with different abilities and backgrounds. When AI is inclusive, it reflects humanity in all its richness. When it is not, it risks reinforcing inequality. Students who study ethical innovation learn that fairness is not an afterthought — it is the foundation of intelligence that benefits all.

Sustainability also plays an important role in building a responsible future. As AI systems require vast amounts of energy, innovators must consider their environmental impact. Ethical innovation seeks balance: creating progress without depleting resources, designing machines that learn efficiently, and supporting the planet that sustains them. This awareness reminds us that intelligence, no matter how advanced, remains a guest of Earth. The future of AI must align with the future of nature.

Teachers can guide students through activities that connect ethics with creativity. For example, they might assign a project where students design an "ethical AI invention," describing not only what it does but how it respects privacy, fairness, and sustainability. These exercises teach that good design includes both engineering and empathy. Ethical innovation, at its core, is about imagining a better world — not just a smarter one.

As society continues to rely on intelligent systems, ethical innovators will become some of the most important leaders of the 21st century. They will work in every field — medicine, education, business, art, and government — ensuring that technology remains a tool for empowerment, not exploitation. They will shape laws, design new models of learning, and inspire communities to think critically about how progress is defined.

The lesson of ethical innovation is timeless: true intelligence must include conscience. The greatest minds in history — from inventors to philosophers — understood that creation without reflection leads to imbalance. In AI, this truth is more urgent than ever. The goal is not to stop progress but to steer it with wisdom, to ensure that every line of code and every spark of discovery carries a trace of compassion.

Innovation gives us the ability to build the future. Ethics gives us the wisdom to build it well. When students learn to join the two, they become more than programmers or engineers — they become architects of hope. Ethical innovation ensures that technology remains guided by humanity, not detached from it. And when that happens, the recipe of intelligence is complete: not only intelligent, but good.

Chapter 14 Summary

Ethical Innovation – Building a Responsible Future

Chapter 14 explains that Artificial Intelligence is one of the most powerful inventions in human history, but with great innovation comes great responsibility. The chapter focuses on ethical innovation, which means creating technology that respects fairness, transparency, inclusivity, sustainability, and human well-being.

The chapter teaches that innovators should not only ask whether technology can be built, but also whether it should be built and who it will serve. AI systems can improve lives, but they can also create harm if they are misused. Examples such as facial recognition, self-driving cars, healthcare AI, and social media algorithms demonstrate how technology requires both technical skill and moral judgment.

Transparency is presented as an important principle of ethical innovation. People should understand how AI systems make decisions. This idea is known as explainable AI, which helps ensure accountability and trust. Inclusivity is another key principle because AI should serve people from all backgrounds, languages, and abilities rather than reinforcing inequality.

The chapter also discusses sustainability and environmental responsibility. Since AI systems require large amounts of energy, innovators must think carefully about how technology impacts the planet. Ethical innovation seeks balance between technological progress and environmental care.

Teachers are encouraged to guide students through projects and discussions that combine creativity with ethics. Students learn that designing responsible technology requires empathy, fairness, and critical thinking. The chapter concludes that true intelligence must include conscience, compassion, and wisdom. Ethical innovation ensures that technology remains guided by humanity and serves the greater good.

Chapter 14 Reflection

This chapter reminds readers that technology should always be guided by ethics and responsibility. Artificial Intelligence has the power to improve healthcare, transportation, education, communication, and many other areas of life. However, if it is created without fairness or compassion, it can also create harm and inequality.

One important lesson from the chapter is that innovation is not only about building smarter machines. It is also about protecting human values such as privacy, fairness, honesty, and respect. Students are encouraged to think critically about the consequences of technology and to consider how AI systems affect people's lives.

The chapter also emphasizes the importance of transparency. People should understand how AI systems make decisions, especially when those decisions impact jobs, healthcare, or safety. Trust in technology grows when systems are clear, explainable, and accountable.

Another important message is that ethical innovation includes everyone. AI should reflect the diversity of humanity and provide equal opportunities for people of different cultures, abilities, and backgrounds. Technology should unite people rather than increase inequality.

Overall, the chapter encourages students to become thoughtful innovators who combine intelligence with compassion. Ethical innovation means building a future where technology serves humanity responsibly and sustainably.

Chapter 14 Worksheet

Part A – Vocabulary

Define the following terms in your own words.

1. Ethical Innovation

___

2. Transparency

___

3. Explainable AI

___

4. Inclusivity

___

5. Sustainability

___

___

Part B – Short Answer Questions

1. Why is ethical innovation important in the development of AI?

2. What questions should innovators ask before building new technology?

3. Why is transparency important in AI systems?

4. How can AI systems become unfair if inclusivity is ignored?

5. Why must innovators consider the environmental impact of AI?

Part C – Critical Thinking

1. Imagine you are designing an AI invention for your school. How would you make sure it is ethical and fair?

2. Do you believe technology companies should be responsible for how people use their AI systems? Explain your answer.

3. How can students help shape a more responsible future with AI?

____
____
____
____

Chapter 14 Quiz

Multiple Choice

1. What is the main focus of ethical innovation?
   A. Building the fastest machines only
   B. Creating technology responsibly and fairly
   C. Removing human involvement
   D. Increasing competition
2. Which concept means people should understand how AI makes decisions?
   A. Automation
   B. Coding
   C. Explainable AI
   D. Virtual Reality
3. Why is inclusivity important in AI?
   A. To limit access to technology
   B. To ensure AI serves diverse people fairly
   C. To increase secrecy
   D. To replace education
4. According to the chapter, sustainability in AI refers to:
   A. Building larger machines
   B. Protecting the environment while advancing technology
   C. Avoiding all innovation
   D. Storing more data
5. Ethical innovators are described as future leaders in:
   A. Only computer science
   B. Every field of society
   C. Sports only
   D. Entertainment only

True or False

6. Ethical innovation asks both "Can we build this?" and "Should we build this?"
   True / False
7. Transparency helps build trust in AI systems.
   True / False
8. AI should only serve the people who create it.
   True / False

9. Sustainability is unimportant in AI development.
   True / False
10. The chapter says true intelligence must include conscience and compassion.
   True / False

Chapter 14 Answer Key

Worksheet Suggested Answers

Part A

Answers will vary.

Part B

1. Ethical innovation helps ensure technology is fair, safe, responsible, and beneficial to humanity.
2. Innovators should ask whether technology should be built, who it will serve, and how it may affect people.
3. Transparency allows people to understand AI decisions and builds accountability and trust.
4. AI can become unfair by excluding certain groups, cultures, or perspectives from data and design.
5. AI systems use large amounts of energy, so innovators must consider environmental sustainability.

Part C

Answers will vary based on student responses.

Quiz Answer Key

1. B. Creating technology responsibly and fairly
2. C. Explainable AI
3. B. To ensure AI serves diverse people fairly
4. B. Protecting the environment while advancing technology
5. B. Every field of society
6. True
7. True
8. False
9. False

10. True

Chapter 15: AI and the Global Community – Intelligence Without Borders

The story of intelligence is no longer confined to one classroom, one country, or one language. It is a story shared by the entire world. Artificial Intelligence has become a global phenomenon — a network of ideas, collaborations, and innovations that connect people across continents. This chapter explores how AI is shaping the **global community**, how nations work together to create it, and how the world must unite to ensure that intelligence serves everyone, not just a few.

AI knows no borders. A translation system built in Japan can help students learn in Brazil. A climate model developed in Germany can predict droughts in Africa. A robot designed in South Korea can assist surgeons in the United States. Each of these achievements shows that intelligence, once local, is now universal. Data travels across oceans, algorithms are shared across research labs, and discoveries are made through cooperation rather than isolation. The global community of AI is a new kind of civilization — one built on shared knowledge and digital connection.

In classrooms around the world, students are discovering that AI is not just a technology but a language — a language that all nations can speak. It is a language of logic, creativity, and problem-solving that transcends geography and culture. A student learning coding in Fiji, Kenya, or France is participating in the same story of discovery. This global exchange of knowledge represents a new chapter in human history — one where education, innovation, and opportunity belong to everyone.

However, this shared kitchen of intelligence comes with challenges. Not every nation has equal access to technology, data, or funding. Some regions lead in AI research, while others struggle to keep pace. This **digital divide** can widen social and economic gaps if left unaddressed. To create true intelligence without borders, countries must invest in education, infrastructure, and inclusivity. Students in developing nations must have the same opportunity to learn coding, use digital tools, and understand AI ethics as those in wealthier nations. Only then can the full potential of global intelligence be realized.

Collaboration between nations is the cornerstone of ethical and sustainable AI. When scientists, engineers, and educators from different backgrounds work together, they bring diverse perspectives that strengthen innovation. A global AI project is like a recipe that draws ingredients from many cultures — each adds a unique flavor that enriches the whole. Shared values such as fairness, transparency, and responsibility become the universal language of this collaboration. In the same way that climate change and health crises demand international unity, the rise of AI calls for a shared global commitment to wisdom and compassion.

Teachers can help students understand global AI by highlighting examples of cooperation. International research teams use AI to monitor endangered species, track pollution, and predict natural disasters. Humanitarian organizations rely on AI to deliver food and medical aid to communities in crisis. During pandemics, data scientists across the world share models to predict infection trends and support public health decisions. These real-world stories show that AI is not just a tool of power — it is a bridge of hope connecting nations in purpose.

Another vital aspect of AI in the global community is cultural preservation. AI can translate ancient languages, digitize historical archives, and help protect endangered traditions. Through careful design, it can amplify voices that have been forgotten and celebrate diversity rather than erase it. When developed with respect and inclusivity, AI becomes a guardian of global heritage — reminding the next generation that progress and identity can coexist.

However, as AI grows more powerful, nations must also guard against misuse. Cyberattacks, misinformation, and surveillance technologies can cross borders as easily as ideas do. This is why **international ethics agreements** and **digital diplomacy** are essential. Just as countries collaborate to prevent war or protect the environment, they must now work together to ensure that AI is used for peace and progress. Students who understand this principle will one day be the diplomats, scientists, and teachers who guide global intelligence with integrity.

The dream of intelligence without borders is not just technological — it is deeply human. It reflects the timeless desire to share knowledge, solve problems, and uplift one another. Every student who learns about AI becomes part of that story. Each new idea, invention, or act of collaboration strengthens the bonds of our global family.

In the end, AI is more than circuits and code; it is a symbol of connection. It shows that when minds unite across distance and difference, humanity grows wiser. The global community of AI is a living example of what happens when we share not only data but dreams. Intelligence without borders is the recipe for a better world — one cooked slowly, with care, courage, and cooperation.

Chapter 15 Summary

AI and the Global Community – Intelligence Without Borders

Chapter 15 explains how Artificial Intelligence has become a global force that connects people, countries, and cultures around the world. AI is no longer limited to one nation or classroom; it is shared through worldwide collaboration, communication, and innovation.

The chapter describes how AI systems developed in one country can help people in another. Translation tools, climate models, medical robots, and global research projects show that intelligence is now shared across borders. Students everywhere are becoming part of a worldwide learning community where coding, creativity, and problem-solving connect people from different cultures and backgrounds.

The chapter also discusses the digital divide. Some nations have greater access to technology, funding, and education, while others struggle to keep pace. To create fairness in the AI age, countries must invest in education, infrastructure, and equal opportunities so all students can participate in the future of technology.

Collaboration is presented as a key ingredient of responsible AI development. Scientists, engineers, educators, and organizations from different nations work together to solve global problems such as climate change, healthcare crises, pollution, and natural disasters. AI becomes a tool not only for innovation but also for humanitarian support and global cooperation.

Another important topic is cultural preservation. AI can help protect languages, traditions, and historical records by digitizing and translating information for future generations. At the same time, the chapter warns that AI can also be misused through cyberattacks, misinformation, and surveillance. This is why global ethics, digital diplomacy, and international cooperation are necessary.

The chapter concludes that intelligence without borders represents humanity working together through shared knowledge, compassion, and cooperation. AI is described not simply as technology, but as a symbol of global connection and shared human progress.

Chapter 15 Reflection

This chapter highlights the importance of global cooperation in the age of Artificial Intelligence. AI has connected nations in ways that were once impossible, allowing people from different cultures to share ideas, solve problems, and support one another. The chapter reminds readers that intelligence grows stronger when knowledge is shared rather than isolated.

One important lesson is that technology should benefit everyone, not just wealthy countries or powerful organizations. Access to education, digital tools, and AI learning opportunities should be available to students around the world. Equality and inclusivity are necessary for a fair technological future.

The chapter also emphasizes that collaboration leads to stronger innovation. When people from different backgrounds work together, they bring unique experiences and perspectives that improve ideas and solutions. Diversity strengthens creativity and problem-solving.

Another important message is that AI must be guided responsibly. Technology can help humanity, but it can also create harm if misused. International ethics and cooperation are essential to protect privacy, prevent misinformation, and ensure that AI supports peace and progress.

Overall, this chapter encourages readers to view AI as a bridge that connects humanity. Intelligence without borders is not only about machines and data — it is about people working together with compassion, wisdom, and shared responsibility for the future.

Chapter 15 Worksheet

Part A – Vocabulary

Define the following terms in your own words.

1. Global Community

2. Collaboration

3. Digital Divide

4. Inclusivity

5. Cultural Preservation

Part B – Short Answer Questions

1. Why does the chapter describe AI as "intelligence without borders"?

2. What is the digital divide, and why is it important to address it?

3. How can international collaboration improve AI systems?

4. Give two examples of how AI can help the global community.

5. Why are international ethics agreements important in the age of AI?

Part C – Critical Thinking

1. How can students around the world benefit from sharing knowledge and technology?

2. Do you think all countries should have equal access to AI education and tools? Why or why not?

3. How can AI help preserve cultures and traditions for future generations?

Chapter 15 Quiz

Multiple Choice

1. According to the chapter, AI has become:
   A. Limited to one country
   B. A global phenomenon
   C. Only for scientists
   D. A local classroom tool
2. What does the digital divide refer to?
   A. Differences in climate
   B. Differences in language

C. Unequal access to technology and education
D. Computer screen sizes

3. The chapter says collaboration between nations strengthens:
   A. Isolation
   B. Innovation
   C. Competition only
   D. Borders
4. Which of the following is an example of AI helping the global community?
   A. Tracking pollution
   B. Building playgrounds only
   C. Replacing teachers entirely
   D. Eliminating culture
5. Why is digital diplomacy important?
   A. To increase misinformation
   B. To ensure AI is used responsibly and peacefully
   C. To stop all technology
   D. To remove international communication

True or False

6. AI systems can help connect people across different countries.
   True / False
7. The chapter says every nation already has equal access to AI technology.
   True / False
8. AI can help preserve languages and cultural traditions.
   True / False
9. International cooperation is unnecessary in the age of AI.
   True / False
10. The chapter describes AI as a symbol of connection and shared progress.
    True / False

Chapter 15 Answer Key

Worksheet Suggested Answers

Part A

Answers will vary.

Part B

1. AI connects people, ideas, and innovations across countries and cultures.
2. The digital divide is unequal access to technology and education, which can create unfair opportunities.
3. Collaboration brings diverse perspectives and improves innovation and ethical development.
4. AI can help track pollution, predict disasters, support healthcare, translate languages, and deliver humanitarian aid.
5. Ethics agreements help ensure AI is used fairly, safely, and responsibly around the world.

Part C

Answers will vary based on student responses.

Quiz Answer Key

1. B. A global phenomenon
2. C. Unequal access to technology and education
3. B. Innovation
4. A. Tracking pollution
5. B. To ensure AI is used responsibly and peacefully
6. True
7. False
8. True
9. False
10. True

Chapter 16: The Learning Mindset – Preparing for an Intelligent World

Every age of discovery begins with a mindset — a way of thinking that allows people to adapt, question, and grow. The age of Artificial Intelligence is no different. As machines learn to recognize patterns, reason, and create, humans must learn something even more powerful: **how to keep learning in an intelligent world.** This chapter explores what it means to have a **learning mindset** in the age of AI — one that values curiosity, adaptability, and the courage to learn alongside machines rather than compete with them.

The learning mindset begins with curiosity. Curiosity is the spark that drives all progress. It asks, "Why?" and "What if?" and "How does this work?" When students approach AI with curiosity instead of fear, they open the door to discovery. They begin to see that AI is not a replacement for human intelligence, but an extension of it — a tool that helps us understand the world more deeply. Curiosity turns technology into a classroom, where every app, robot, or dataset becomes a teacher.

Adaptability is the second pillar of the learning mindset. In a world where technology evolves faster than ever, what we know today may change tomorrow. The most successful learners will not be those who memorize the most facts, but those who can **learn, unlearn, and relearn** with confidence. Teachers can help students develop adaptability by encouraging experimentation — letting them try new coding languages, explore creative projects, or work through failure. In this new age, mistakes are not setbacks; they are stepping stones to growth.

Critical thinking forms the third pillar. As AI systems generate information, images, and answers, students must learn to question them. They must ask: *Is this accurate? Who created it? What assumptions are behind it?* Critical thinking turns information into insight. It allows young minds to separate truth from error, originality from imitation, and logic from manipulation. In a world where machines generate content in seconds, human judgment becomes more valuable than ever.

Empathy is another vital part of the learning mindset. As AI takes on more roles in society, humans must remember the emotional intelligence that sets them apart. Machines can analyze words but not feel kindness; they can predict outcomes but not understand pain. Students who practice empathy will grow into leaders who guide technology with care. They will design AI that respects privacy, includes diverse voices, and serves the greater good. Empathy ensures that intelligence always serves humanity, not the other way around.

In classrooms, the learning mindset can be cultivated through creativity and collaboration. Students can work on group projects that mix art, science, and ethics — writing stories about AI futures, building models that solve community problems, or debating how AI should make decisions. These experiences teach that intelligence thrives when shared. When students learn from one another, they mirror the very essence of AI — a system that grows stronger through connection and feedback.

The learning mindset also embraces **lifelong education**. AI will change jobs, industries, and ways of living, but it will never replace the human capacity to learn new skills. Students today will have careers that do not yet exist. To prepare for that future, they must see learning as a continuous journey, not a destination. The best learners will be explorers — unafraid to step into new fields, confident in their ability to grow with change.

Teachers play a powerful role in nurturing this mindset. They are the gardeners of curiosity, planting seeds of wonder in every lesson. When they use AI tools in the classroom, they model how technology can empower rather than intimidate. They show that learning with machines is not about competition but partnership — a shared quest for knowledge. Teachers who encourage questioning and creativity prepare students not just for exams, but for life in an intelligent world.

The learning mindset also invites humility. AI may surpass humans in speed or precision, but humans remain unmatched in imagination and moral reasoning. Understanding this balance helps students respect technology without idolizing it. It reminds them that even as machines grow more capable, the human heart remains the true source of innovation. The future belongs to those who can think critically, feel deeply, and learn endlessly.

Preparing for an intelligent world means preparing the mind and spirit to evolve. It means realizing that knowledge is not fixed — it flows, adapts, and expands. Every generation must learn how to learn again, just as every machine must train before it performs. The difference is that humans can choose to learn with empathy and purpose.

The learning mindset is not just a skill — it is a way of living. It encourages curiosity in the face of uncertainty, resilience in the face of failure, and kindness in the face of progress. It transforms fear of technology into fascination, and competition into collaboration. Students who carry this mindset into the future will not be overwhelmed by AI — they will be empowered by it. They will not see machines as rivals, but as partners in the endless adventure of discovery.

Chapter 16 Summary

The Learning Mindset – Preparing for an Intelligent World

Chapter 16 explains that success in the age of Artificial Intelligence depends on developing a strong learning mindset. A learning mindset is a way of thinking that encourages curiosity, adaptability, critical thinking, empathy, and lifelong learning. The chapter teaches that humans should learn alongside machines rather than fear or compete with them.

Curiosity is described as the spark that drives discovery. Students who ask questions and explore how technology works become better learners and innovators. Adaptability is another important skill because technology changes quickly. Students must learn how to adjust, experiment, and continue learning throughout life.

Critical thinking helps students question AI-generated information and determine whether it is accurate, trustworthy, and ethical. Empathy is also essential because machines cannot truly understand human emotions or kindness. Human compassion ensures that AI systems are created responsibly and used for the benefit of society.

The chapter also highlights creativity, collaboration, and lifelong learning. Students are encouraged to work together, solve problems, and explore new ideas across subjects such as science, ethics, and art. Teachers are recognized as important guides who nurture curiosity and help students learn how to use AI responsibly.

Finally, the chapter explains that the future belongs to learners who can think critically, adapt to change, and continue growing throughout life. A learning mindset transforms fear into curiosity and turns technology into a tool for discovery and progress.

Chapter 16 Reflection

This chapter reminds us that learning is not something that ends after school. In the age of Artificial Intelligence, learning is a lifelong journey. Technology will continue to change the world, which means people must continue to grow, adapt, and stay curious.

One of the most important lessons in this chapter is that students should not fear AI. Instead, they should learn how to use it wisely and responsibly. AI can support creativity, research, communication, and problem-solving, but humans must guide it with ethics and empathy.

The chapter also teaches that mistakes are part of learning. Failure should not discourage students because every mistake provides an opportunity to improve and grow stronger. Adaptability and resilience are essential skills in an intelligent world.

Another important message is that human qualities such as kindness, imagination, and moral reasoning remain irreplaceable. Machines may process information quickly, but humans provide purpose, compassion, and ethical judgment.

Overall, this chapter encourages readers to remain curious, open-minded, and willing to learn throughout life. The learning mindset is not only about education — it is about becoming a thoughtful, responsible, and compassionate human being in a rapidly changing world.

Chapter 16 Worksheet

Part A – Vocabulary

Define the following terms in your own words.

1. Curiosity

____

2. Adaptability

____

3. Critical Thinking

____

4. Empathy

____

5. Lifelong Learning

____

____

Part B – Short Answer Questions

1. Why is curiosity important in the age of AI?

2. What does the chapter mean by "learn, unlearn, and relearn"?

3. Why is critical thinking important when using AI-generated information?

4. How does empathy help guide technology responsibly?

5. According to the chapter, how can teachers help students prepare for an intelligent world?

Part C – Critical Thinking

1. Describe a situation where adaptability could help someone succeed in the future workplace.

2. How can students balance technology use with human values like kindness and empathy?

3. Do you believe AI should be viewed as a competitor or a partner? Explain your answer.

____

____

____

____

Chapter 16 Quiz

Multiple Choice

1. What is the first pillar of the learning mindset discussed in the chapter?
   A. Competition
   B. Curiosity
   C. Speed
   D. Programming
2. Adaptability means the ability to:
   A. Avoid change
   B. Memorize everything
   C. Learn and adjust to change
   D. Ignore technology
3. Why is critical thinking important in the age of AI?
   A. To make machines faster
   B. To question and evaluate information
   C. To replace teachers
   D. To avoid learning
4. According to the chapter, empathy helps students:
   A. Build larger machines
   B. Understand emotions and guide AI responsibly
   C. Program robots faster
   D. Memorize data
5. The chapter describes teachers as:
   A. Builders of machines
   B. Gardeners of curiosity
   C. Computer operators
   D. Software engineers

True or False

6. The chapter says mistakes are stepping stones to growth.
   True / False
7. AI can fully replace human empathy and compassion.
   True / False
8. Lifelong learning is important in an intelligent world.

9.
   True / False
10. Students should fear AI because it will replace all human learning.
   True / False
11. The learning mindset encourages collaboration instead of competition.
   True / False

Chapter 16 Answer Key

Worksheet Suggested Answers

Part A

Answers will vary.

Part B

1. Curiosity encourages discovery, questioning, and learning about technology.
2. It means people must continue adapting and learning new skills as technology changes.
3. Critical thinking helps students evaluate whether information is accurate, trustworthy, and ethical.
4. Empathy helps people design and use AI systems that respect humanity and fairness.
5. Teachers guide students by encouraging curiosity, creativity, ethical thinking, and responsible technology use.

Part C

Answers will vary based on student responses.

Quiz Answer Key

1. B. Curiosity
2. C. Learn and adjust to change
3. B. To question and evaluate information
4. B. Understand emotions and guide AI responsibly
5. B. Gardeners of curiosity
6. True
7. False
8. True
9. False
10. True

Chapter 17: Closing Reflections – The Human Heart of the Machine

Every great creation carries the spirit of its maker. Behind every code, circuit, and algorithm lies the quiet presence of human thought — the hand that built it, the mind that imagined it, and the heart that gave it purpose. Artificial Intelligence, though made of silicon and logic, reflects the best and worst of the people who design it. This chapter is a reflection — a gentle pause at the end of our exploration — to remind students and teachers that the future of AI will always depend on the *heart of humanity* that guides it.

When we began this book, we compared intelligence to a kitchen — a place where ingredients blend to create something greater than the sum of its parts. We studied data as the raw ingredient, algorithms as the recipe, models as the learners, chips as the tools, and energy as the flame. We saw how human knowledge acts as the chef's wisdom — the guiding force that gives flavor and direction. Now, as we reach the final page, we see that the most essential ingredient of all has no formula. It is empathy — the ability to care, to imagine, to understand, and to love.

Machines can learn to calculate but not to care. They can generate poetry, but not feel beauty. They can predict a smile, but not experience joy. That difference — small but immeasurable — is what makes humanity extraordinary. In a world surrounded by machines, the most intelligent act may be the simplest one: to remain human.

For students, this reflection is an invitation. You are entering a world where intelligence will surround you — in classrooms, workplaces, and homes. AI will help you learn, create, and dream. But never forget that it learns from you, too. Every question you ask, every discovery you make, shapes the intelligence of tomorrow. The systems you will build one day will mirror your values, your empathy, and your imagination. Use that power wisely. Build not only for progress, but for people.

For teachers, this closing chapter is both gratitude and encouragement. You are the architects of understanding — the ones who show young minds that technology is not something to fear, but something to guide with integrity. When you teach students about AI, you are not merely teaching them how machines think. You are teaching them how *humans should think* in an age of extraordinary possibility. You remind them that knowledge without ethics is incomplete, and that innovation without compassion is hollow. You prepare them not just for exams, but for a future where wisdom will be as essential as code.

The heart of the machine is not made of metal or electricity — it is made of meaning. Every AI system begins with a human idea: a desire to solve, to understand, to connect. That desire is what gives machines purpose. Without it, they are silent tools; with it, they become instruments of discovery. Students who see this connection will realize that the boundary between human and artificial intelligence is not a wall but a mirror. What we build reflects who we are.

As AI grows more powerful, the world will face questions that have no easy answers. What should machines be allowed to decide? How much data should they access? How do we keep innovation fair, sustainable, and just? The answers will not come from algorithms alone. They will come from people — thinkers, dreamers, teachers, and students — who understand that intelligence without conscience is incomplete.

Artificial Intelligence is not the end of the human story; it is a new chapter in our evolution. It challenges us to grow wiser, kinder, and more curious. It asks us to reimagine education, to blend science with ethics, and to view technology not as a threat, but as a companion in the journey of knowledge.

The future belongs to those who can balance logic with love, and computation with compassion. Machines may help us reach the stars, but only humanity can give those stars meaning.

And so, the recipe of intelligence ends where it began — in the heart.
For it is there that all true learning begins, and where every great creation finds its purpose.

Chapter 17 Summary

Closing Reflections – The Human Heart of the Machine

This chapter reminds readers that Artificial Intelligence is ultimately a reflection of humanity. Behind every AI system are human beings who create, guide, and shape its purpose. Throughout the book, intelligence was compared to a kitchen where ingredients work together: data acts as the raw ingredient, algorithms as recipes, models as learners, chips as tools, and energy as the flame. Yet the chapter concludes that the most important ingredient is empathy — the human ability to care, understand, and imagine.

The chapter explains that machines can calculate, predict, and generate information, but they cannot truly feel emotions, beauty, love, or joy. This difference is what makes humans unique. Students are encouraged to use AI wisely and remember that the systems they create in the future will reflect their own values, ethics, and imagination.

Teachers are recognized as guides who help students understand technology responsibly. Education is described as more than teaching machines or coding; it is about teaching wisdom, ethics, integrity, and compassion in a rapidly changing world.

The chapter also highlights that future AI challenges — such as fairness, privacy, and decision-making — cannot be solved by machines alone. Humanity must guide technology with conscience and responsibility. The chapter closes with the idea that intelligence begins and ends in the human heart, where meaning, empathy, and purpose are created.

Chapter 17 Reflection

Artificial Intelligence may continue to grow more powerful, but this chapter reminds us that human values will always matter most. Machines can assist people, but they cannot replace empathy, kindness, imagination, or moral judgment. As students and future leaders, it is important to understand that technology should improve human life rather than control it.

This chapter also teaches that education is not only about learning technical skills. It is about developing wisdom, responsibility, and ethical thinking. Teachers play an important role in helping students understand how to use technology in ways that are fair, compassionate, and meaningful.

The closing message of the chapter encourages readers to think carefully about the future they want to create. AI is not separate from humanity — it reflects humanity. The systems people build tomorrow will mirror the values they choose today. The future belongs to those who can balance intelligence with empathy and innovation with humanity.

Chapter 17 Worksheet

Part A – Vocabulary

Define the following terms in your own words.

1. Empathy

___

2. Ethics

___

3. Artificial Intelligence

___

4. Innovation

___

5. Compassion

___

___

Part B – Short Answer Questions

1. According to the chapter, why is empathy considered the most important ingredient of intelligence?

___

___

___

2. What does the chapter mean when it says AI reflects humanity?

3. Why are teachers important in the age of Artificial Intelligence?

4. What are some questions society must answer as AI becomes more powerful?

5. Explain the meaning of the statement: "The future belongs to those who can balance logic with love."

Part C – Critical Thinking

1. If you could design an AI system to help people, what would it do and why?

2. How can students make sure they use AI responsibly?

3. Do you believe technology should always be guided by human values? Explain your answer.

Chapter 17 Quiz

Multiple Choice

1. What does the chapter describe as the most important ingredient of intelligence?
   A. Data
   B. Algorithms
   C. Empathy
   D. Energy
2. According to the chapter, machines can calculate but cannot:
   A. Learn
   B. Process information
   C. Care
   D. Analyze data
3. Teachers are described as:
   A. Programmers of machines
   B. Architects of understanding
   C. Builders of robots
   D. Designers of chips
4. The chapter says AI systems reflect:
   A. Only technology
   B. Random information
   C. Human values and ideas
   D. Electricity
5. Which of the following is a future challenge mentioned in the chapter?
   A. Choosing favorite colors
   B. Building larger classrooms
   C. Deciding how much data AI should access
   D. Printing more books

True or False

6. Machines can truly experience human emotions.
   True / False
7. AI is described as a new chapter in human evolution.
   True / False
8. Knowledge without ethics is complete.
   True / False
9. The chapter encourages students to use AI responsibly.
   True / False
10. The chapter ends by emphasizing the importance of the human heart.
   True / False

Chapter 17 Answer Key

Worksheet Suggested Answers

Part A

Answers will vary.

Part B

1. Empathy allows humans to care, understand others, and use intelligence responsibly.
2. AI reflects the values, ideas, and decisions of the humans who create it.
3. Teachers help students understand technology with ethics, wisdom, and responsibility.
4. Society must answer questions about fairness, privacy, ethics, and decision-making.
5. It means people should combine intelligence and technical skills with kindness and compassion.

Part C

Answers will vary based on student responses.

Quiz Answer Key

1. C. Empathy
2. C. Care
3. B. Architects of understanding
4. C. Human values and ideas
5. C. Deciding how much data AI should access
6. False
7. True
8. False
9. True
10. True

The AI Ingredient Family – A Summary of Harmony

Every recipe depends on balance. Each ingredient, no matter how small, plays a role in the success of the whole. Artificial Intelligence is built the same way — a blend of families that work together to form a complete system of thought, learning, and creation. When combined, they form not just a machine that thinks, but a living symbol of how knowledge, technology, and humanity can work together.

At the heart of the family stands **The Data Family**, the gatherers and storytellers of information. They collect the raw ingredients of intelligence — numbers, words, images, and sounds — that represent the experiences of the world. Without them, there would be no foundation for learning. Data teaches AI what the world looks like, what people value, and how patterns connect one event to another. But data alone is silent; it needs structure and interpretation to speak.

That is where **The Algorithm Family** enters — the thinkers and planners. They are the designers of logic, transforming raw information into understanding. Algorithms decide how to read, sort, and connect data, turning chaos into order. Like chefs with precise recipes, they organize the steps of learning and guide AI toward insight. Their creativity lies not in the data itself, but in how they choose to shape it.

From there, **The Model Family** begins its work. These are the learners — the students of the digital world. Models take the lessons of the algorithms and refine them through experience. They practice, test, and improve. Over time, they develop intuition — the ability to predict, recognize, and respond to new situations. A model's strength lies in its adaptability; it grows wiser with each encounter, reminding us that all learning, human or artificial, is a journey of patience and feedback.

Behind the scenes, **The Chip Family** provides the hands and tools that make intelligence possible. Chips, processors, and circuits are the silent builders of the AI world. They perform the calculations, store the memories, and sustain the flow of energy that keeps everything moving. Without them, intelligence would remain an idea — beautiful, but motionless. They are the architects of speed and precision, turning imagination into performance.

Powering them all is **The Energy Family** — the heartbeat of creation. Energy fuels every action, every computation, every decision. It flows through the circuits of machines the way blood flows through living beings. The Energy Family reminds us that intelligence, like life, requires care, conservation, and respect for the natural world. Without energy, even the most brilliant idea remains dormant. With it, thought becomes motion, and motion becomes understanding.

And at the center of it all stands **The Human Family** — the creators, teachers, and moral guardians. Humanity gives AI its purpose, its direction, and its soul. The Human Family teaches machines not only how to think but *why* to think. It provides the wisdom to balance curiosity with conscience, innovation with empathy, and power with humility. Humans are not separate from AI; they are its designers, guides, and companions in the pursuit of knowledge.

Together, these six families form a complete ecosystem — a network of collaboration where each part depends on the others. When the Data Family gathers, the Algorithm Family interprets. When the Model Family learns, the Chip Family enables it. When the Energy Family powers the system, the Human Family ensures it serves life. Intelligence emerges not from competition, but from harmony — from the same cooperation that sustains nature, science, and civilization itself.

The lesson of the AI Ingredient Family is simple but profound: progress is never built alone. Every discovery is a collaboration between idea and effort, structure and imagination, machine and mind. As students learn from these families, they are not only studying technology — they are learning the art of balance. They see that intelligence, in every form, thrives when knowledge and kindness grow together.

Artificial Intelligence, when guided by these families, becomes more than a tool; it becomes a mirror of humanity's best qualities — curiosity, creativity, and compassion. The family of intelligence is a reflection of our own. It reminds us that we are all connected — in thought, in energy, and in purpose — building a world where learning never ends and understanding never stops growing.

Benefits for Students – Growing with the Ingredients of Intelligence

Learning about Artificial Intelligence is more than studying computers; it is learning how thinking itself works. For students, *The Ingredients of AI* opens the door to curiosity, creativity, and confidence in a world shaped by technology. Each chapter invites young learners to explore how data, algorithms, and human wisdom connect to create modern intelligence.

Students who study this book gain **a foundation for the future.** They learn that AI is not magic — it is logic, design, and discovery. Understanding how AI functions helps students develop critical-thinking skills. They begin to question how decisions are made, how machines learn, and how ethics protect fairness. These lessons build a mindset that goes beyond technology — a mindset of awareness and responsibility.

This book also strengthens **problem-solving and imagination.** By comparing intelligence to a kitchen of ingredients, students visualize complex systems in a simple, creative way. They begin to see patterns in everything — in science, in art, and in life. Each concept teaches that learning is not memorizing facts, but understanding relationships.

Most importantly, *The Ingredients of AI* helps students discover their own voice in the intelligent world. They see that they can be inventors, coders, writers, or artists — all guided by the same curiosity that drives innovation. It teaches them that technology should never replace humanity but should serve it. Every student who reads this book carries forward a new belief: that intelligence begins with kindness, grows through learning, and shines brightest when shared.

Benefits for Teachers – Guiding the Next Generation of Thinkers

For teachers, *The Ingredients of AI* offers a bridge between traditional education and the new era of digital understanding. It provides a structured, ethical, and creative way to introduce complex technological ideas in language students can grasp. The book transforms classrooms into laboratories of thought, where discussion, experimentation, and imagination thrive together.

Teachers who use this book can integrate AI literacy across multiple subjects — science, mathematics, language, and social studies. Each chapter connects theory with real-world relevance, encouraging dialogue about technology's impact on daily life. Lessons on algorithms can become writing exercises on fairness; chapters on neural networks can inspire art projects about how the brain learns.

This book also helps teachers cultivate **ethical awareness** in students. It emphasizes privacy, empathy, and responsibility as inseparable parts of innovation. When teachers guide students through these topics, they nurture not only digital literacy but moral literacy — preparing young minds to become thoughtful digital citizens.

Most importantly, *The Ingredients of AI* honors the teacher's timeless role as mentor. It positions educators not as bystanders to technology, but as leaders in shaping its use. Teachers become the moral architects of the intelligent classroom — showing students how to balance logic with compassion and knowledge with humility.

Comprehension and Reflection Quiz

The following quiz is designed to help students reflect on what they've learned throughout the book. It can be used for class discussion, short essays, or group projects. Teachers may adapt the questions to fit grade levels or learning objectives.

Part I – Understanding the Ingredients

1. Explain how data functions as the "raw ingredient" of intelligence. Why is data quality important in AI systems?
2. Describe how algorithms and models work together to help machines learn. What would happen if either one were missing?
3. What role does energy play in AI, and how does it relate to sustainability?
4. How does human wisdom guide the development of AI systems? Provide an example from your own experiences.
5. In what ways does creativity make AI systems more powerful and more human-like at the same time?

Part II – Ethical and Social Reflection

6. Why is data privacy essential in protecting individuals in the digital world?
7. Discuss one example of ethical innovation. How does it combine progress with responsibility?
8. How can countries work together to build intelligence "without borders"?
9. What is the difference between machine intelligence and human consciousness?
10. In your opinion, what is the most important ingredient of AI, and why?

Part III – Personal Growth and Critical Thinking

11. How has this book changed your understanding of Artificial Intelligence?
12. Which chapter inspired you the most, and what lesson will you carry into your future learning?

13. How can empathy and curiosity help you become a better student in the age of AI?
14. Imagine you are designing your own AI system. What would it do, and how would you make sure it helps people?
15. Describe what it means to have a "learning mindset." How can this attitude help you adapt to an intelligent world?

Teacher Reflection Prompt

After students complete the quiz, invite them to reflect as a class:
How can humans and machines learn *together*? What does it mean to build intelligence that serves humanity instead of replacing it?

Partner, with these three sections — **Student Benefits, Teacher Benefits, and the Quiz** — your book *The Ingredients of AI* is now fully complete, balanced, and classroom-ready for district submission or publishing layout.

How to Use This Book in the Classroom

The Ingredients of AI was designed not only as a reading experience but as a **teaching framework** — a guide for exploring Artificial Intelligence through creativity, ethics, and understanding. Each chapter builds upon the one before it, allowing teachers to move naturally from foundational ideas to advanced reflection. Whether used in middle school, high school, or early college, this book transforms the classroom into an environment of curiosity and discovery.

For Teachers

Teachers can use each chapter as a **stand-alone lesson** or as part of a complete unit. The "kitchen of intelligence" metaphor — with its families of Data, Algorithm, Model, Chip, Energy, and Human Wisdom — gives students an easy way to visualize how AI systems function. Chapters can be read aloud, discussed, or paired with interactive demonstrations. For example, while reading about data and algorithms, students might collect classroom data and create a simple rule-based activity to mimic how machines learn from examples. When studying ethics or privacy, they can debate real-world case studies.

The book's tone encourages **discussion rather than memorization**. Teachers are invited to pause after each section, ask reflective questions, and connect AI concepts to everyday experiences. Lessons can blend with English, Social Studies, or Art to show that AI is not just a technical subject — it is part of human culture and creativity.

Teachers can also use the **Comprehension and Reflection Quiz** at the end of the book as a formative assessment or a guided writing exercise. The quiz questions are designed not only to test knowledge but to invite critical thinking and empathy. Students can respond individually or in small groups, creating collaborative discussions about what responsible intelligence means.

Finally, teachers are encouraged to use the **Benefits pages** as inspiration for classroom goals. The "Benefits for Students" section highlights growth in problem-solving, ethical reasoning, and creativity. The "Benefits for Teachers" page supports professional development, showing how AI education strengthens modern teaching methods.

For Students

Students can approach this book as both a science text and a story about the future. Each chapter can be read independently or in sequence. Teachers may assign journal reflections, short essays, or creative projects based on each theme.
Students might illustrate the "AI Family" as a visual poster, write a poem about the "Secret Ingredient," or create a short presentation explaining how human and machine collaboration works in real life.

The book's writing style is designed for **deep reading** — paragraphs instead of bullet points — encouraging students to engage with language and comprehension. They are asked to think, not just remember. Each chapter closes with questions that can lead to classroom dialogue or writing prompts.

Interdisciplinary Integration

Because AI connects to every field, this book can be woven into multiple subjects:

- **Science & Technology:** Study the mechanics of learning, data, and algorithms.
- **Language Arts:** Analyze the narrative metaphors of "kitchen," "recipe," and "family."
- **Social Studies:** Discuss global cooperation, ethics, and digital citizenship.
- **Art & Design:** Visualize the AI Family through drawings, posters, or creative projects.
- **Philosophy & Ethics:** Reflect on consciousness, fairness, and human responsibility.

By combining disciplines, teachers show that Artificial Intelligence is not a distant subject — it is the story of how learning, creativity, and technology unite.

For Classroom Outcomes

By the end of this course or reading program, students should be able to:

1. Explain the core components of Artificial Intelligence using real-world examples.

2. Describe how data, algorithms, and models interact to form intelligent systems.
3. Discuss ethical and global issues surrounding AI with understanding and empathy.
4. Identify how AI impacts their daily lives and future careers.
5. Demonstrate a learning mindset — the ability to think critically, question deeply, and adapt to change.

Final Note to Educators

This book was written to make AI education inclusive and inspiring. It honors teachers as mentors and students as explorers. Every page aims to remind readers that intelligence — in machines or in people — thrives where curiosity and compassion meet.

By teaching *The Ingredients of AI*, you are not just preparing students for the future of technology; you are preparing them to **shape it**.

Glossary

Letter A

1. Access Time

The amount of time it takes for an AI system or computer to locate and retrieve data from memory or storage. Access time affects how quickly megabytes of data can be used during AI processing.

2. Activation Data

Intermediate data generated inside an AI model while it is running. Activation data is stored temporarily in memory and often measured in megabytes during model execution.

3. Adaptive Storage

A storage approach that automatically adjusts how data is stored or moved based on usage patterns. In AI systems, adaptive storage helps manage large volumes of megabytes efficiently.

4.Algorithm

An algorithm is a set of logical steps used to solve a problem or perform a task. In AI, algorithms act like the recipe that tells the system how to use data to reach a goal. Some algorithms help sort information, while others help machines recognize faces, predict trends, or translate languages.

The strength of an algorithm lies in its design — clear, fair, and efficient instructions make learning both powerful and ethical.

5. Algorithmic Data Size

The total amount of data an algorithm needs to operate effectively. In AI, this size is often measured in megabytes or larger units, depending on model complexity.

6. Allocation (Memory Allocation)

The process of assigning a specific number of megabytes in memory or storage for an AI task, model, or dataset.

7. Analytics Dataset

A structured collection of data used for analysis or AI training. The size of an analytics dataset is commonly measured in megabytes, gigabytes, or more.

8. Annotation Storage

The space required to store labels, tags, or explanations added to AI training data. These annotations contribute additional megabytes to total dataset size.

9.Artificial Intelligence (AI)

Artificial Intelligence is the branch of computer science that enables machines to perform tasks that normally require human intelligence. These tasks include learning, reasoning, perception, and problem-solving. AI systems process information, recognize patterns, and make decisions using data. The goal of AI is not to replace human intelligence but to extend it — to create machines that assist, inspire, and collaborate with people. In simple terms, AI is the science of teaching machines how to think and learn from experience.

10. Artificial Neural Network (ANN) Size

The total memory footprint of a neural network, including weights, biases, and parameters. ANN size is often described in megabytes when discussing model efficiency.

11. Asset Compression

The process of reducing the number of megabytes required to store AI-related files such as models, images, or datasets without losing essential information.

12. Available Memory

The amount of free memory, measured in megabytes, that an AI system can still use to load data, run models, or perform computations.

13.ANI (Artificial Narrow Intelligence)

Artificial Narrow Intelligence refers to AI systems designed to perform **one specific task or a narrow set of tasks** rather than general intelligence. ANI systems rely on data stored and processed in memory and storage measured in **megabytes, gigabytes, or more**. Examples include image recognition, speech-to-text, recommendation systems, and chatbots. ANI does not understand beyond its training scope, but it can process large amounts of data efficiently within its defined function.

Letter B

1. Bandwidth

The amount of data that can be transferred between systems in a given time. In AI systems, bandwidth determines how quickly megabytes of data can move between storage, memory, and processors.

2. Batch Processing

A method where AI systems process large groups of data all at once instead of one item at a time. Batch processing often involves handling many megabytes of data in a single operation.

3.Bias

Bias occurs when an AI system produces unfair or unbalanced results because of the data it was trained on. If data reflects human prejudice, the AI may learn and repeat it. For example, a hiring algorithm trained on biased historical records may favor certain groups over others. Recognizing and correcting bias ensures that AI decisions are fair and inclusive.

4. Binary Encoding

The process of representing information using binary values (0s and 1s). All megabytes of AI data are ultimately stored and transmitted using binary encoding.

5. Bit Depth

The number of bits used to represent a single piece of data, such as a pixel or audio sample. Higher bit depth increases data quality but also increases the number of megabytes required.

6. Bitmap Data

A type of image data where each pixel is stored as a set of bits. Bitmap images can quickly grow in size, consuming large numbers of megabytes in AI vision systems.

7. Buffer Memory

Temporary memory used to hold data while it is being transferred or processed. Buffers store data in chunks measured in megabytes to keep AI systems running smoothly.

8. Bulk Data Storage

Large-scale storage designed to hold massive datasets used for AI training or analysis. Bulk storage capacity is measured in megabytes, gigabytes, or larger units.

9. Byte Stream

A continuous flow of bytes transmitted or processed by a system. AI applications often analyze byte streams that accumulate into megabytes of data.

10. Bytecode

An intermediate form of program code that is easier for machines to execute than human-written code. Bytecode files occupy storage space measured in megabytes.

11. Byzantine Fault Tolerance (BFT)

A system property that allows AI or distributed systems to continue functioning even when some components fail or act unpredictably. Implementing BFT requires additional data handling and storage overhead measured in megabytes.

Letter C

1. Cache Memory

A small, high-speed memory area that stores frequently used data so the processor can access it faster. Cache helps reduce the time needed to move megabytes of data from main memory or storage.

2. Capacity Planning

The process of estimating how much memory and storage an AI system will need. Capacity planning ensures there are enough megabytes available to handle data, models, and future growth.

3. Checkpoint File

A saved snapshot of an AI model during training. Checkpoint files are stored in memory or storage and often consume many megabytes so training can resume without starting over.

Chip (Processor)

A chip is the hardware brain of AI — a small but powerful piece of technology that performs calculations at incredible speeds. Chips come in different types: **CPUs** handle general tasks, **GPUs** process visual data and large computations, and **TPUs** (Tensor Processing Units) are specialized for AI learning. The chip family provides the strength and structure that turns algorithms into action, making it possible for intelligence to exist in machines.

4. Chunking

The practice of breaking large datasets into smaller pieces. Chunking helps AI systems process megabytes of data more efficiently by handling them in manageable parts.

5. Cloud Storage

A method of storing data on remote servers accessed through the internet. Cloud storage manages files measured in megabytes and allows AI systems to scale beyond local hardware limits.

6.Collaboration

Collaboration between humans and machines is one of the most important themes in modern AI. It means working together — combining human creativity with machine precision. When people and technology cooperate, they produce results neither could achieve alone. Collaboration turns AI into a partner, not a rival, in the continuous journey of discovery.

7. Compression

The process of reducing the size of data so it uses fewer megabytes. Compression helps AI systems store, transfer, and process data more efficiently.

8. Compute Load

The amount of processing work required to run an AI task. Compute load often increases as the number of megabytes being processed grows.

9.Consciousness

Consciousness is the awareness of being — the ability to experience, feel, and reflect. While AI can simulate understanding, it does not possess consciousness. It can analyze emotion but cannot feel it. The study of consciousness in AI helps students explore what it means to be truly alive and aware — reminding us that machines may learn to think, but only humans can dream.

10. Context Window

The amount of data an AI model can consider at one time. Context windows consume memory measured in megabytes, especially in language and vision models.

11. Corpus

A large collection of text or data used to train AI models. A corpus is usually measured in megabytes or larger units depending on its size.

12. CUDA Memory

Specialized memory used by GPUs to accelerate AI computations. CUDA memory holds model data and intermediate results measured in megabytes during processing.

Cybersecurity

Cybersecurity is the protection of computer systems and networks from unauthorized access, theft, or damage. It acts like a lock on the doors of the digital world. In AI, cybersecurity prevents hackers from manipulating data or models. Encryption, strong passwords, and secure connections help maintain trust in intelligent systems. Without cybersecurity, even the brightest technologies remain vulnerable.

Letter D

Data

Data is the raw ingredient of intelligence — the digital form of knowledge that machines use to learn. Every photo, sound, word, or number stored on a device becomes part of a larger recipe that feeds AI systems. When data is gathered, cleaned, and organized, it transforms into meaningful information. Just as chefs need quality ingredients, AI systems depend on accurate and diverse data to produce reliable results.

1. Data Allocation

The process of assigning a specific amount of memory or storage for data use. In AI systems, data allocation determines how many megabytes are reserved for datasets, models, or tasks.

2. Data Buffer

A temporary storage area that holds data while it is being transferred or processed. Data buffers manage megabytes of information to keep AI systems running smoothly.

3. Data Compression

A technique used to reduce the size of data so it consumes fewer megabytes. AI systems use data compression to save storage space and speed up data transfer.

4. Data Footprint

The total amount of data an AI system uses, including datasets, models, and temporary files. A data footprint is measured in megabytes, gigabytes, or more.

5. Data Loader

A software component that loads data into memory for AI training or inference. Data loaders handle batches of data measured in megabytes.

6. Data Migration

The process of moving data from one storage system to another. During AI system upgrades, data migration may involve transferring large numbers of megabytes.

Data Privacy

Data privacy is the right to control how personal information is collected, shared, and used. In the digital world, every piece of data — from a photo to a fingerprint — represents part of someone's identity. Ethical AI systems respect privacy by asking for consent, securing information, and using data only for its intended purpose. Privacy protection ensures that the recipe of intelligence remains safe and respectful to all.

7. Data Throughput

The rate at which data is processed or transferred by a system. Higher throughput allows AI systems to move more megabytes efficiently.

8. Dataset Size

The total amount of data in a dataset used for AI training or testing. Dataset size is commonly measured in megabytes or larger units.

Deep Learning

Deep learning is a form of machine learning that uses large neural networks to process complex data. It allows AI to analyze millions of examples and discover hidden relationships without being explicitly programmed. Deep learning powers many familiar technologies — from voice assistants to self-driving cars — by helping machines understand images, sounds, and languages with remarkable accuracy.

9. Deep Learning Model Size

The amount of memory required to store a deep learning model, including its parameters and weights. Model size is often described in megabytes to assess efficiency.

10. Disk Storage

Long-term storage used to save files, datasets, and AI models. Disk storage capacity and usage are measured in megabytes, gigabytes, or terabytes.

Letter E

1. Edge Computing

A computing approach where data is processed closer to where it is generated rather than sent to a central server. Edge computing reduces how many megabytes must be transferred over networks.

2. Embedding Size

The amount of memory required to store vector representations used by AI models. Embedding size is often measured in megabytes and affects model performance and storage needs.

3. Encoded Data

Data that has been converted into a specific format for storage or transmission. Encoded data occupies megabytes depending on the encoding method used.

4. Encoding Scheme

A rule set that defines how data is represented digitally, such as text or images. Different encoding schemes can increase or reduce the number of megabytes required.

5. Encrypted Storage

Storage that protects data by converting it into a secure format. Encryption may slightly increase the number of megabytes used due to added security information.

6. End-to-End Data Pipeline

The full path data takes from collection to processing and storage. Each stage of the pipeline manages data volumes measured in megabytes.

7.Energy

Energy is the invisible force that powers every form of intelligence. Without it, even the smartest systems remain silent. In AI, energy fuels chips, servers, and data centers. It turns motion into memory and code into creation. The more advanced AI becomes, the more efficiently it must use energy. Sustainable innovation ensures that the growth of intelligence does not come at the expense of the planet.

8. Energy Efficiency (AI Systems)

A measure of how much energy an AI system uses to process data. Systems that move and store fewer megabytes are often more energy efficient.

9.Ethics in AI

Ethics in AI is the study of how to make intelligent systems fair, transparent, and beneficial to humanity. It asks questions about what machines should do, not just what they can do. Ethical AI avoids bias, respects privacy, and promotes accountability. It ensures that progress is guided by conscience, making technology not only intelligent but also humane.

10. Execution Memory

The memory required while a program or AI model is running. Execution memory usage is tracked in megabytes during runtime.

10. External Storage

Storage devices located outside a computer, such as USB drives or external hard drives. External storage capacity is measured in megabytes and larger units.

11. Extracted Features

Important data patterns identified by AI models during processing. Extracted features are stored temporarily or permanently in memory measured in megabytes.

Letter F

1. Feature Map

A structured output produced by AI models, especially in image and signal processing. Feature maps are stored in memory and can consume significant megabytes during computation.

2. Feature Scaling

The process of adjusting data values to a consistent range before training an AI model. Feature scaling affects how efficiently megabytes of data are processed and stored.

3. File Allocation Table (FAT)

A file system structure that tracks where files are stored on a disk. FAT helps manage how megabytes are organized and retrieved from storage.

4. File Compression Format

A standardized way to reduce file size so it uses fewer megabytes. Compression formats help AI systems store and transfer data efficiently.

5. File System Cache

A temporary memory area that stores frequently accessed files. File system caches reduce repeated access to storage and manage megabytes more efficiently.

6. Floating-Point Data

Numerical data that includes decimal values and is commonly used in AI calculations. Floating-point data requires more bits per value, increasing memory usage measured in megabytes.

7. Frame Buffer

A region of memory that stores image or video frames before they are displayed or processed. Frame buffers often consume large numbers of megabytes in AI vision systems.

8. Fragmentation

A condition where data is stored in scattered locations instead of one continuous block. Fragmentation can reduce storage efficiency even when megabytes appear available.

9. Free Memory

The amount of unused memory available for programs or AI tasks. Free memory is measured in megabytes and determines how much additional data can be loaded.

10. Full Dataset Load

The act of loading an entire dataset into memory at once. This approach can require large amounts of megabytes and is common in AI training scenarios.

Letter G

1. Garbage Collection

An automatic memory-management process that frees memory no longer in use. Garbage collection helps reclaim megabytes so AI programs can continue running efficiently.

2. Generalization Data

Data used to test how well an AI model performs on new, unseen inputs. Storing and evaluating generalization data requires additional megabytes beyond training data.

3.Gigabyte (GB) A larger unit of data measurement equal to 1,024 megabytes (or commonly approximated as 1,000 MB). Gigabytes are used when datasets or models grow beyond megabyte scale.

4.Global Intelligence

Global intelligence is the shared effort of nations, cultures, and communities to build technology that serves humanity. It reflects the idea that intelligence has no borders — that data, ideas, and compassion can travel freely across the world. When people collaborate through AI, they transform technology into a universal language of hope and progress.

5. Graph Data Structure

A way of organizing data using nodes and connections. Graph-based AI systems store graph data in memory and storage measured in megabytes.

6. GPU Memory

Specialized memory used by graphics processing units to accelerate AI workloads. GPU memory holds model parameters and data batches measured in megabytes.

7. Gradient Data

Numerical values calculated during AI training to update model parameters. Gradient data is stored temporarily in memory and contributes to overall megabyte usage.

8. Granularity

The level of detail at which data is stored or processed. Finer granularity often increases the number of megabytes required.

9. Greedy Algorithm

An algorithm that makes the best immediate choice at each step. Greedy algorithms may reduce memory usage by limiting how many megabytes of data must be stored at once.

10. Ground Truth Data

Correct, labeled data used to train or evaluate AI systems. Ground truth datasets are stored in files measured in megabytes or larger units.

11. Growth Rate (Data)

The speed at which data size increases over time. In AI systems, a high data growth rate means storage needs measured in megabytes can expand quickly.

Letter H

1. Hard Disk Capacity

The total amount of data a hard disk can store. Capacity is measured in megabytes and larger units.

2. Hardware Acceleration

The use of specialized hardware to speed up AI processing. Acceleration often reduces how long megabytes of data stay in memory.

3. Hash Table

A data structure that stores information for fast lookup. Hash tables occupy memory measured in megabytes in large AI systems.

4. Hierarchical Storage

A storage design that uses multiple layers such as RAM, disk, and cloud. Each layer manages data measured in megabytes.

5. High-Dimensional Data

Data with many features or variables. High-dimensional datasets often require large numbers of megabytes.

6. Host Memory

Main system memory used by the CPU. Host memory stores AI data and models measured in megabytes.

7.Human Wisdom

Human wisdom is the final ingredient in the recipe of intelligence. It is the moral compass that guides invention. Wisdom cannot be coded or downloaded; it is earned through experience, empathy, and reflection. AI may one day help us process information faster, but wisdom reminds us why we seek knowledge in the first place — to improve life, preserve beauty, and honor one another.

8. Hybrid Storage

A combination of different storage types working together. Hybrid storage systems manage megabytes across multiple devices.

9. Hyperparameter Storage

Memory used to store configuration values for AI models. These settings are saved in files measured in megabytes.

10. Hyperscale Data

Extremely large datasets used by major AI systems. Hyperscale data is tracked from megabytes up to much larger units.

11. Heuristic Data

Information used by AI systems to guide decision-making. Heuristic data contributes to the overall data size in megabytes.

Letter I

1. Image Dataset Size

The total amount of storage required for image data. Size is measured in megabytes or more.

2. Inference Memory

The memory used when an AI model is making predictions. Inference memory usage is tracked in megabytes.

3. Input Buffer

A temporary area where incoming data is stored. Input buffers hold megabytes before processing begins.

4. Intermediate Data

Data produced during processing steps. Intermediate data can significantly increase memory usage in megabytes.

5. Index File

A file that helps locate data quickly. Index files use additional megabytes to improve performance.

6. Information Density

The amount of useful data stored within a given size. Higher density means more information per megabyte.

7. Initialization Data

Data loaded when an AI system starts. Initialization data occupies memory measured in megabytes.

8. In-Memory Processing

Processing data directly in RAM instead of storage. This approach uses large amounts of m

9.Innovation

Innovation is the process of transforming ideas into reality. In AI, innovation means designing systems that improve lives, expand knowledge, and solve problems ethically. True innovation does not rush ahead without reflection; it grows with responsibility and purpose. It is the balance of imagination and discipline — the heartbeat of progress.

emory measured in megabytes.

10. Input Feature Size

The amount of data required to represent input features. Feature size affects how many megabytes are needed.

11. Instruction Cache

A small memory area that stores frequently used instructions. Instruction caches manage small but critical megabytes.

Letter J

1. Job Queue

A list of tasks waiting to be processed. Job queues may store task data measured in megabytes.

2. Joint Dataset

A dataset created by combining multiple sources. Joint datasets often increase total size in megabytes.

3. JSON Data Size

The amount of storage required for data stored in JSON format. JSON files can grow quickly in megabytes.

4. Jitter Buffer

A temporary storage area that smooths data flow. Jitter buffers store megabytes during real-time processing.

5. Job Scheduler

A system that decides when tasks run. Schedulers manage memory and data measured in megabytes.

6. Just-in-Time Processing

Processing data only when needed. This approach can reduce how many megabytes are stored at once.

7. Joint Memory Allocation

Memory shared across multiple AI tasks. Joint allocation must carefully manage available megabytes.

8. Java Bytecode Size

The storage size of compiled Java programs. Bytecode files occupy megabytes on disk.

9. Job Metadata

Information describing AI tasks. Metadata adds additional megabytes to total system storage.

10. Junction Storage Point

A logical link between storage locations. Junctions help organize data measured in megabytes.

Letter K

1. Kernel Memory

Memory reserved for core system operations. Kernel memory usage is tracked in megabytes.

2. Key-Value Store

A data storage method that pairs keys with values. Large key-value stores consume many megabytes.

3. Knowledge Base Size

The total amount of stored knowledge in an AI system. Size is measured in megabytes or larger units.

4. K-Means Dataset Size

The amount of data used in clustering algorithms. Dataset size affects memory usage in megabytes.

5. Keras Model Size

The storage required for AI models built with Keras. Model size is measured in megabytes.

6. Keyframe Data

Important frames selected from video data. Keyframe storage contributes to total megabyte usage.

7. Kernel Cache

A cache used by the operating system kernel. Kernel caches store frequently used data in megabytes.

8. Knowledge Graph Storage

Memory used to store relationships between data points. Knowledge graphs require significant megabytes.

9. Kinetic Data Stream

Continuously changing data from sensors or systems. These streams generate growing megabytes over time.

10. K-Nearest Neighbor Memory Usage

The memory required by nearest-neighbor algorithms. Memory use increases as datasets grow in megabytes.

Letter L

1. **Latency**
   The delay between requesting data and receiving it. Latency affects how quickly megabytes move through AI systems.
2. **Layer Output Size**
   The amount of data produced by a neural network layer. Output size is measured in megabytes during processing.
3. **Learning Mindset**
4. The learning mindset is the ability to grow, adapt, and remain curious in an intelligent world. It values questioning over memorization and sees failure as part of discovery. Students with a learning mindset are prepared not only for AI but for life — they learn how to learn, how to evolve, and how to shape the future with courage and creativity.
5.
6. **Load Balancing**
   Distributing work across systems so no single device is overloaded. Balancing helps manage megabytes efficiently.
7. **Local Storage**
   Data stored on a device rather than the cloud. Local storage capacity is measured in megabytes.
8. **Log File Size**
   The amount of storage used by system logs. Logs can accumulate many megabytes over time.
9. **Loss History Data**
   Stored values showing how model error changes during training. Loss history consumes megabytes.
10. **Low-Precision Data**
    Data stored using fewer bits per value. Low-precision formats reduce megabyte usage.
11. **Labeled Dataset**
    Data that includes tags or labels for AI training. Labels increase total dataset size in megabytes.
12. **Linear Model Size**
    The storage required for a linear AI model. Size is measured in megabytes.

13. **Load Time**
    The time required to bring data or models into memory. Load time depends on megabytes involved.

Letter M

Machine Learning (ML)

Machine Learning is a branch of AI that enables computers to learn from data instead of being programmed step by step. Through experience, the system identifies patterns and improves its performance over time. Just as students learn by practicing and making mistakes, machines learn by analyzing examples and refining their understanding. ML is the science of teaching machines to learn the way humans do — through repetition, correction, and curiosity.

1. **Memory Allocation**
   Assigning a specific amount of memory for tasks. Allocation is tracked in megabytes.
2. **Memory Footprint**
   The total memory an AI program uses. Footprint is measured in megabytes.
3. **Metadata Size**
   The storage used by descriptive information about data. Metadata adds extra megabytes.
4. **Mini-Batch Size**
   The amount of data processed at once during training. Batch size affects megabyte usage.
5. **Model**
6. A model is what an AI system becomes after it learns from data. It represents the system's understanding of patterns and relationships. For example, a speech recognition model learns to nderstand words by analyzing thousands of voices. A model is like the finished dish that results from following the recipe — shaped by data, refined by algorithms, and constantly improving with feedback.

7. **Model Checkpoint Size**
   The storage required for saved training states. Checkpoints often consume many megabytes.
8. **Model Compression**
   Reducing model size while preserving performance. Compression lowers megabytes required.
9. **Model Parameters**
   Values learned by an AI model. Parameter storage contributes to total megabytes.
10. **Memory Bandwidth**
    The rate at which memory transfers data. Bandwidth affects how fast megabytes move.

11. **Multimodal Dataset**
    Data combining text, images, audio, or video. Multimodal data uses large megabytes.
12. **Mutable Data**
    Data that changes during processing. Mutable data can increase temporary megabyte usage.

Letter N

1. **Network Bandwidth**
   The capacity of a network connection. Bandwidth controls how many megabytes can be transferred.
2. **Neural Network**
3. A neural network is a digital structure inspired by the human brain. It consists of layers of interconnected nodes called "neurons," which process and pass information. Each connection strengthens as the system learns, much like the way the brain builds memory through experience. Neural networks allow AI to recognize complex patterns — such as faces, voices, or emotions — making them the foundation of modern deep learning.

4. **Neural Network Size**
   The total storage required for a neural network. Size is measured in megabytes.
5. **Node Memory**
   Memory available on a computing node. Node memory limits megabytes per task.
6. **Normalization Data**
   Values used to scale data consistently. Normalization adds to dataset megabytes.
7. **Non-Volatile Memory**
   Memory that retains data without power. Capacity is measured in megabytes.
8. **Numerical Precision**
   The detail level of stored numbers. Higher precision increases megabytes.
9. **Noise Data**
   Unwanted or random information in datasets. Noise increases data size in megabytes.
10. **Neural Activation Size**
    Memory used to store neuron outputs. Activation size is measured in megabytes.
11. **Network Transfer Size**
    The amount of data sent across a network. Transfer size is tracked in megabytes.
12. **Node Cache**
    Temporary storage on a node for faster access. Cache size uses megabytes.

Letter O

1. **Object Storage**
   A storage method that manages data as objects. Capacity is measured in megabytes.
2. **Offline Dataset**
   Data stored locally rather than streamed. Offline datasets occupy megabytes.
3. **On-Device Storage**
   Storage located on the AI device itself. On-device capacity is measured in megabytes.
4. **Operational Memory**
   Memory used during active AI operations. Usage is tracked in megabytes.
5. **Optimization Data**
   Information used to improve model performance. Optimization data uses megabytes.
6. **Output Buffer**
   Temporary storage for results before delivery. Buffers hold megabytes.
7. **Overhead Data**
   Extra data required for system operation. Overhead increases total megabytes.
8. **Object Detection Output Size**
   The amount of data produced by detection models. Output size is measured in megabytes.
9. **Online Storage**
   Storage accessible via the internet. Online storage limits are measured in megabytes.
10. **Open Dataset Size**
   The storage footprint of publicly available datasets. Size is measured in megabytes.

Letter P

1. **Parameter Count**
   The total number of model values. Count correlates with megabytes required.
2. **Persistent Storage**
   Long-term storage that retains data. Capacity is measured in megabytes.
3. **Pipeline Buffer**
   Temporary storage between processing stages. Buffers manage megabytes in motion.
4. **Preprocessing Data**
   Data created while preparing datasets. Preprocessing adds megabytes.
5. **Precision Reduction**
   Lowering numeric detail to save space. Reduction decreases megabyte usage.
6. **Prediction Output Size**
   The amount of data produced by model predictions. Size is measured in megabytes.
7. **Primary Memory**
   Main system memory used for processing. Capacity is measured in megabytes.
8. **Processing Overhead**
   Extra resources needed during computation. Overhead increases megabyte usage.
9. **Profiling Data**
   Information collected to analyze performance. Profiling data uses megabytes.
10. **Paged Memory**
   Memory divided into fixed-size blocks. Paging manages megabytes efficiently.

Letter Q

1. **Quantization**
   A technique that reduces numerical precision to lower memory usage. Quantization helps AI models use fewer megabytes.
2. **Query Cache**
   Stored results from previous searches or requests. Query caches save megabytes by avoiding repeated computation.
3. **Query Latency**
   The time it takes to retrieve data after a request. Latency depends on how many megabytes must be accessed.
4. **Queue Buffer**
   A temporary holding area for data waiting to be processed. Buffers store megabytes in order.
5. **Quick Access Memory**
   Memory designed for fast retrieval. It handles megabytes needed immediately by AI tasks.
6. **Quantitative Dataset**
   Data made up of numerical values. These datasets are stored and measured in megabytes.
7. **Quantum Computing**
8. Quantum computing represents the next frontier of intelligence. Unlike classical computers that use bits (0 or 1), quantum computers use **qubits**, which can represent both 0 and 1 at the same time. This allows them to perform many calculations simultaneously, unlocking new possibilities in medicine, climate research, and AI learning. Quantum AI is like a new kitchen — one that cooks with atoms instead of electricity, using the laws of physics to explore infinite possibilities.
9. **Query Result Size**
   The amount of data returned from a query. Result size is measured in megabytes.
10. **Quorum Storage**
    A distributed storage method requiring agreement across systems. Data is replicated in megabytes.
11. **Quality Metrics Data**
    Information used to measure model performance. Metrics consume storage in megabytes.
12. **Quantized Model Size**
    The reduced size of an AI model after quantization. Size is typically measured in megabytes.

Letter R

1. **RAM Usage**
   The amount of active memory in use. RAM usage is tracked in megabytes.

2. **Read Throughput**
   The speed at which data is read from storage. Throughput affects how fast megabytes are accessed.
3. **Real-Time Processing**
   Processing data immediately as it arrives. Real-time systems manage megabytes continuously.
4. **Recursive Memory Use**
   Memory consumption during repeated function calls. Usage accumulates in megabytes.
5. **Redundant Storage**
   Extra copies of data kept for reliability. Redundancy increases total megabytes stored.
6. **Resource Allocation**
   Assigning system resources like memory and storage. Allocation is measured in megabytes.
7. **Runtime Memory**
   Memory required while a program is running. Runtime memory usage is tracked in megabytes.
8. **Raw Dataset Size**
   The size of unprocessed data. Raw datasets often require many megabytes.
9. **Read-Only Memory Footprint**
   The storage space used by non-modifiable data. Footprint is measured in megabytes.
10. **Retrieval Speed**
    How quickly stored data can be accessed. Speed depends on the number of megabytes involved.

Letter S

1. **Sample Size**
   The number of data examples used in AI training. Larger samples increase megabytes.
2. **Scalable Storage**
   Storage that grows with demand. Scalability supports increasing megabytes.
3. **Serialized Data Size**
   The storage size of data converted into a transferable format. Size is measured in megabytes.
4. **Shared Memory**
   Memory accessible by multiple processes. Shared memory usage is tracked in megabytes.
5. **Snapshot Size**
   The storage required for saved system states. Snapshots consume megabytes.
6. **Sparse Data Representation**
   A storage method that saves space when data contains many empty values. Sparsity reduces megabytes.
7. **Storage Capacity**
   The total amount of data a system can store. Capacity is measured in megabytes or more.
8. **Streaming Data Buffer**
   Temporary storage for incoming data streams. Buffers handle megabytes in motion.
9. **System Cache**
   Memory that stores frequently used data. Caches manage megabytes for faster access.

10. **Synchronization Data**
    Information used to keep systems aligned. Sync data adds to total megabytes.

Letter T

1. **Temporary Storage**
   Short-term storage used during processing. Temporary storage holds megabytes briefly.
2. **Tensor Size**
   The memory required to store multidimensional data structures. Tensor size is measured in megabytes.
3. **Throughput Rate**
   The amount of data processed per unit time. Rate is often described in megabytes per second.
4. **Training Dataset Size**
   The total amount of data used to train AI models. Size is measured in megabytes.
5. **Transfer Buffer**
   Temporary memory used during data movement. Buffers hold megabytes during transfer.
6. **Transactional Storage**
   Storage that ensures data consistency. Transactions add overhead measured in megabytes.
7. **Thread Memory Usage**
   Memory consumed by execution threads. Usage is tracked in megabytes.
8. **Token Storage Size**
   The memory required to store processed tokens. Token data uses megabytes.
9. **Time-Series Data Size**
   The storage footprint of data collected over time. Size increases in megabytes.
10. **Training Checkpoint Size**
    The storage required for saved training states. Checkpoints are measured in megabytes.

Letter U

1. **Unified Memory**
   A memory system shared between CPU and GPU. Unified memory manages data in megabytes efficiently across processors.
2. **Upload Size**
   The amount of data sent to storage or the cloud. Upload size is measured in megabytes.
3. **User Data Storage**
   Storage allocated for user-generated files. Capacity is tracked in megabytes.
4. **Utilization Rate**
   The percentage of memory or storage currently in use. Utilization reflects how many megabytes are occupied.
5. **Uncompressed Data Size**
   The size of data before compression. Uncompressed data often uses more megabytes.

6. **Update Payload**
   Data sent during software or model updates. Payload size is measured in megabytes.
7. **Uptime Storage Logs**
   Logs recorded while systems run continuously. Logs accumulate megabytes over time.
8. **Unified Dataset**
   A dataset combined from multiple sources. Size is measured in megabytes.
9. **User Session Memory**
   Memory allocated for active users. Session memory uses megabytes dynamically.
10. **Usage Quota**
    A storage limit set for users or systems. Quotas are defined in megabytes or larger units.

Letter V

1. **Validation Dataset Size**
   The amount of data used to evaluate AI models. Size is measured in megabytes.
2. **Vector Embedding Size**
   The memory required to store numerical representations of data. Size is measured in megabytes.
3. **Virtual Memory**
   A system that extends RAM using disk storage. Virtual memory is managed in megabytes.
4. **Volatile Memory**
   Memory that loses data when power is off. Capacity is measured in megabytes.
5. **Video Dataset Size**
   The storage required for video data. Video datasets consume many megabytes.
6. **Versioned Storage**
   Storage that keeps multiple file versions. Versioning increases megabyte usage.
7. **Vision Model Size**
   The memory footprint of computer vision models. Size is measured in megabytes.
8. **Vector Database Storage**
   Storage used for similarity search data. Vector databases consume large megabytes.
9. **Virtualized Storage**
   Storage abstracted from physical hardware. Capacity is tracked in megabytes.
10. **Volume Capacity**
    The total size of a storage volume. Capacity is measured in megabytes or more.

Letter W

1. **Weight Parameters**
   Learned values in AI models. Weight storage contributes to megabytes used.

2. **Working Memory**
   Memory actively used during processing. Working memory usage is measured in megabytes.
3. **Write Throughput**
   The speed at which data is written to storage. Throughput affects megabytes per second.
4. **Warm Cache**
   Cached data that is already loaded. Warm caches reduce repeated megabyte transfers.
5. **Workflow Data Size**
   The total data used across an AI workflow. Size is measured in megabytes.
6. **Web Dataset Size**
   The storage required for web-based data. Size is tracked in megabytes.
7. **Weight Compression**
   Reducing model weight size to save memory. Compression lowers megabytes used.
8. **Window Size (AI Context)**
   The amount of data processed at once. Window size affects memory megabytes.
9. **Writable Storage**
   Storage that allows data modification. Capacity is measured in megabytes.
10. **Workload Memory Demand**
    The memory required for tasks. Demand is expressed in megabytes.

Letter X

1. **X-Axis Data Size**
   Data stored along one dimension of a dataset. Size contributes to megabytes used.
2. **XML Data Size**
   The storage footprint of XML-formatted data. XML files often use many megabytes.
3. **XOR Encoding**
   A binary operation used in data processing. Encoded data occupies megabytes.
4. **Execution Context Size**
   Memory required during task execution. Size is measured in megabytes.
5. **External Dataset Size**
   The size of data sourced externally. External datasets add megabytes.
6. **Expanded Memory Use**
   Memory growth during processing. Expansion increases megabytes consumed.
7. **Experimental Dataset**
   Data used for testing AI models. Size is measured in megabytes.
8. **Extraction Buffer**
   Temporary storage during data extraction. Buffers store megabytes briefly.
9. **Extended Storage Capacity**
   Additional storage added to a system. Capacity is measured in megabytes.
10. **Explainability Data Size**
    Data used to explain AI decisions. Explainability outputs consume megabytes.

Letter Y

1. **Yield Data Size**
   The amount of useful output data produced. Yield is measured in megabytes.
2. **Yearly Data Growth**
   Annual increase in stored data. Growth is tracked in megabytes.
3. **YAML File Size**
   The storage footprint of YAML configuration files. Size is measured in megabytes.
4. **Y-Axis Feature Size**
   Feature data along a dataset dimension. Size contributes to megabytes.
5. **Young Generation Memory**
   Memory area for newly created data. Usage is measured in megabytes.
6. **Yield Optimization Data**
   Data used to improve output efficiency. Stored in megabytes.
7. **YourAIStudyBuddy Dataset Size**
   The total data used by AI study tools. Size is measured in megabytes.
8. **Yottabyte Reference Scale**
   A conceptual upper scale of data measurement. Used for comparison beyond megabytes.
9. **Yield Metrics Storage**
   Storage used for performance metrics. Metrics consume megabytes.
10. **Yoked Memory Allocation**
    Linked memory regions used together. Allocation is measured in megabytes.

Letter Z

1. **Zero-Copy Memory**
   A method that avoids duplicating data. Zero-copy reduces megabytes in motion.
2. **Zipped Dataset Size**
   The storage size after compression. Zipped files use fewer megabytes.
3. **Zettabyte Scale (Reference)**
   A large-scale data concept. Used to compare growth beyond megabytes.
4. **Zone-Based Storage**
   Storage divided into regions. Zones manage megabytes efficiently.
5. **Z-Score Normalization Data**
   Statistical values used in preprocessing. Data adds megabytes.
6. **Zero Padding**
   Adding placeholder data to inputs. Padding increases memory megabytes.
7. **Zoomed Feature Maps**
   Scaled representations in vision models. Stored in megabytes.
8. **Zonal Cache**
   Cache divided by region. Cache size is measured in megabytes.
9. **Zero-Day Model Update Size**
   The storage required for emergency updates. Size is measured in megabytes.
10. **Zipped Model Archive**
    Compressed AI model files. Archives reduce megabytes required.

NOTES:

NOTES:

NOTES:

NOTES:

NOTES:

www.ingramcontent.com/pod-product-compliance
Ingram Content Group UK Ltd.
Pitfield, Milton Keynes, MK11 3LW, UK
UKHW062013041026
15591UKWH00017B/1312

9 781972 925096